Wild Wire™

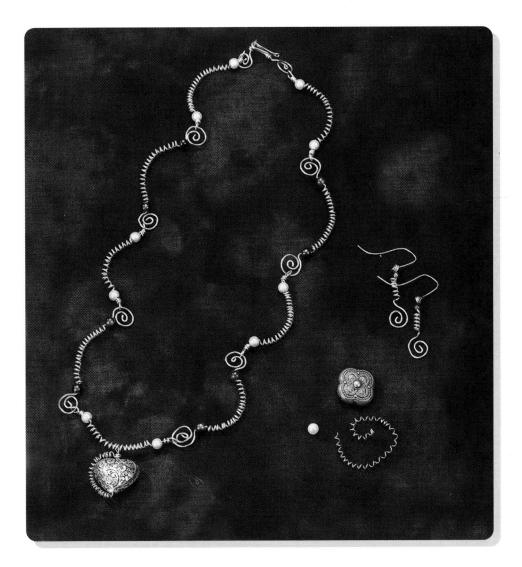

NSi™
Innovations

Published by

krause publications

700 East State Street • Iola, WI 54990-0001
715/445-2214 • FAX: 715/445-4087   www.krause.com

Please call or write for our free catalog of publications. Our toll-free number to place an order or obtain a free catalog is 800-258-0929 or please use our regular business telephone 715-445-2214.

Library of Congress Catalog Number 2001099546
ISBN 0-87349-457-1

Warning: Wire has functional sharp points.
Warning: Choking hazard; small parts. The tools and materials in this book are not intended for use by children.
When cutting wire, wear safety goggles.
The Original Be-Dazzler Stud and Rhinestone Setting Machine™ is intended for adult use.

Introduction

It wasn't but a few years ago that wire was barely present in the craft and art worlds; sure, it was used to make ear wires for earrings and to link beads together for other jewelry applications, but not until recently have we begun to truly explore its uses and discover its awesome versatility.

Consequently, it is easy to forget that wire has a long, rich history that dates back to ancient and medieval times, when it was used to adorn Egyptian sarcophagus and as protective chain-mail for European knights. Over the following centuries, it was used as personal adornment, as seen in the amazing jewelry from such far-off lands as Morocco, and utilitarian items, like rug beaters and baskets.

Throughout the ages, wire has proven to be an infinite source of wonder, and this continues to be true even today as we learn how to shape, coil, and form it into nearly any configuration imaginable. This book aims to give you the basic techniques for starting your own journey of discovery with wire. We have provided more than 60 projects to be a springboard for creativity; however, if you don't like an aspect of a project, change the color of wire, use different beads, or even alter the jig pattern, for example, to make it uniquely yours.

For more information on NSI Innovations Wild Wire™ products, visit www.nsiinnovations.com, the company's website.

Be Creative and Have Fun!

Table of Contents

Wild Wire
Supplies and Basic Techniques 6

Be-Dazzler
Supplies and Basic Techniques 18

Section 1

Projects for You 22

Double
Coil Bracelet,
Page 27.

Section 2

Projects for Your Home 68

Fleur de lis
Bottle, Page 79.

Section 3

Projects for Giving and Preserving Memories 90

Thanks a
Whole Bunch
Card, Page 92.

Wild Wire

Supplies and Basic Techniques

Wire is one of the most versatile art and craft mediums currently available. With a few turns of a pliers, or a wrap on a jig, you can make an incredible array of jewelry, home décor, and paper projects, ranging in style from whimsical to sophisticated.

Before starting any of the projects in this book, please take the time to review the information on the following pages; not only will you get an introduction to wire and the vast selection of tools you can use to create with it, but you will also learn the basic techniques needed to successfully complete all of the projects in this book. Even if you have worked with wire before, it never hurts to brush up on the basics!

Supplies

The basic supplies, materials, and tools needed to create with wire are widely available. Don't be tempted to walk into your hardware store and pick up wire and pliers; make sure you work with tools and supplies that are specifically designed for use in the craft and art worlds! A "standard" pliers may have grooves on the tips that will mar and mark your wire, and more "industrial" wires may be too difficult to work with or have coatings on them that are not satisfactory for a project's end use.

Wire

Craft wire is available in various colors and weights. The higher the gauge number, the thinner the wire. For the projects in this book, we recommend a wire that falls between 16 gauge and 22 gauge, although wire is available through the very thin 28 gauge. Practice with a few different gauges and see which works best for you for your particular project.

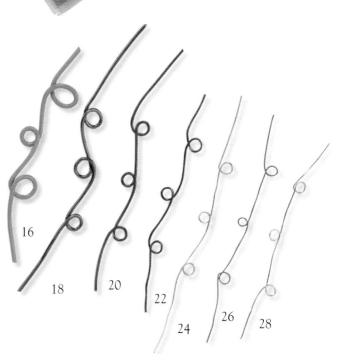

16
18
20
22
24
26
28

Wire in various gauges, from the heavy 16 gauge to the thin 28.

Pliers

Round Nose Pliers are the most basic tool in wire craft. The nose of these pliers is made up of two tapered round metal tips that grasp and bend the wire. As you squeeze the handles together, you close the gap between the tips of the nose. Many round nose pliers also have a wire cutter, found just under the nose. To use the wire cutter, spread the handles open and slip the wire inside the cutter. Squeeze the handles together to cut.

Bent Chain Nose Pliers allow you to grasp and manipulate the wire a little more easily, especially with smaller, more intricate areas.

Flat Nose Pliers have angular tips. This type of pliers can be used to create sharp angles in the wire as well as grip and bend it.

Nylon Jaw Pliers are great for smoothing out wire. If the wire you are using gets little bends or kinks in it, place the bent part of the wire between the jaws of these pliers and press down to straighten it out. Because of the nylon coating, these pliers will not scratch or damage the wire.

Other Tools and Supplies

Beads, both glass and frosted, add a touch of elegance to your wire creations. You can add these beads to coiled wire beads, or you can simply string them onto wire.

Files are used to smooth out the tip of the wire if it is sharp.

Round Nose Pliers.

Flat Nose Pliers.

Bent Chain Nose Pliers.

Nylon Jaw Pliers.

Files.

Assorted Glass and Frosted Beads.

A **Jig** is a platform on which you can design and shape wire. Pegs, which come in four sizes, fit into the holes of the jig and are arranged depending on the shape you wish to create. Moving the position of the pegs changes the shape of the wire, and changing the size of the peg affects the size of the resulting loop.

A **Nylon Hammer** will gently flatten areas in your design; this gives added strength to finished pieces. Hitting the wire harder will give it a unique look.

The **Twist n' Curl** will allow you to make different kinds of coiled beads with wire. The tool comes with a handle and an assortment of rods, each creating a different size and shape of coil.

Besides just cutting wire, **Wire Cutters** help you snip in areas that may be hard to reach. They will enable you to trim off small ends that would not otherwise fit inside of your regular pliers. When cutting, always aim the wire away from your face or other people! When cutting a small piece of wire, hold the wire in an enclosed area such as a trash bin. It is always recommended to wear safety goggles when cutting wire.

The **Wire Writer** is a unique tool that is to be used with a jig. It allows you to literally write with wire! Use the tool to write your name or a message and apply it to nearly any surface for a unique look.

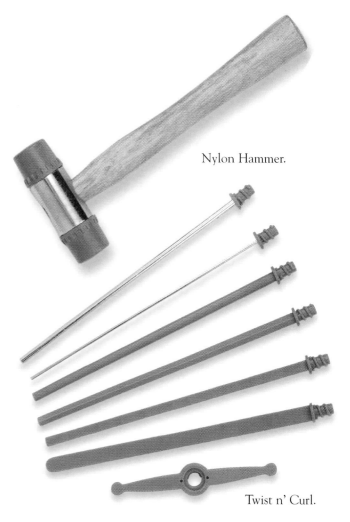

Nylon Hammer.

Twist n' Curl.

Jig and pegs.

Wire Cutter.

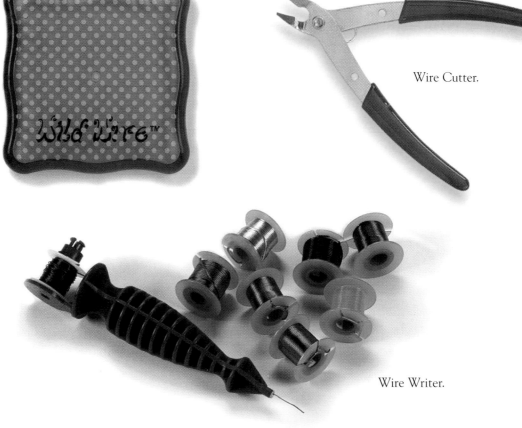

Wire Writer.

Techniques

While we know you are anxious to get started creating cool jewelry, home décor items, and paper projects, please read the following section and practice the basic techniques before you begin any of the projects in this book.

Creating an Anchor Loop

This loop starts off most shapes in wire craft and is also used as an anchor loop on a jig. Practice this technique until you have mastered it!

1. Grip an end of wire between the nose of the round nose pliers. The wire should be positioned about 1/4" down from the tip of the nose. Squeeze the handles of the pliers and keep a tight grip on the wire.

2. Carefully wind the wire around the nose of the pliers one turn, creating a tight loop. This can be done by either turning the pliers or by pulling the wire around.

3. Pull the loop off of the nose of the pliers, then place the looped end between the tips of the pliers and squeeze to flatten out the end. This is very important, because the end sticking out is sharp and can scratch you, so you will need to flatten it. If necessary, you can file the end to smooth it.

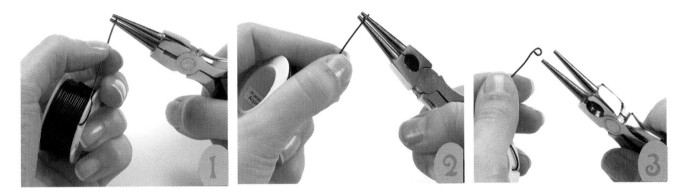

Wire Jump Rings

Completed shapes can be easily attached to each other with small wire jump rings. See page 87 for a fast way to make multiple jump rings.

1. Create an anchor loop.

2. Using the wire cutter, trim off the straight end of the wire under the loop. The pliers can then be used to open the ring so that it can be attached to another wire shape.

3. Use the pliers again to squeeze the ring closed.

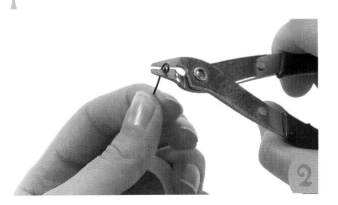

A bead link is any number of beads on wire with a loop at each end; these loops are a variation of the anchor loop and are called eye loops. Bead links can be attached to each other, forming a chain, or they can be attached to other wire shapes.

1 To create an eye loop, make an anchor loop. Now grip the loop inside the nose of the round nose pli-ers and turn it slightly to center it over the straight end of the wire.

2 Slide beads onto the straight end of the wire after the loop.

3 Cut off the excess wire after the last bead, leaving 3/8" of wire. Create another loop with the 3/8" end of wire, flattening the end and centering the loop as in Step 1.

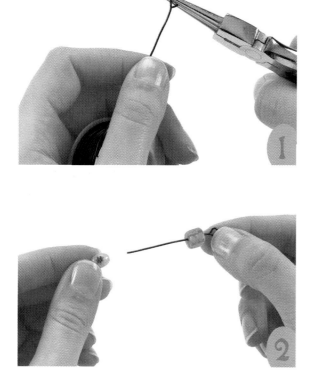

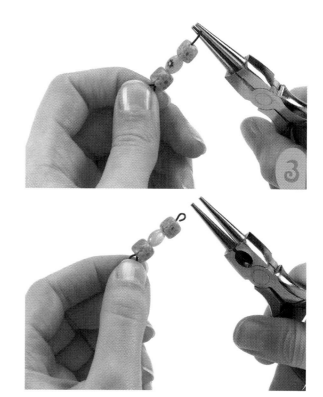

You will be using a basic spiral in many of the projects in this book.

1 Make an anchor loop at the end of the wire.

2 Grip the loop between the jaws of the nylon jaw pliers. Begin to circle the wire around the loop.

3 Shift the position of the loop as you circle the wire around. Repeat until you have created a spiral of desired width.

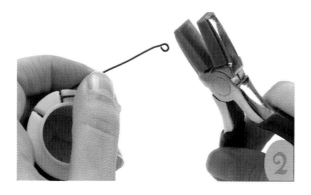

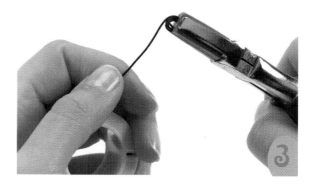

This unique spiral can be used to add interesting lines to your projects.

1 Using the bent chain nose pliers, bend the wire at a right angle, starting about 1/2" from one end.

2 Continue to bend and shape the wire at right angles, moving the pliers along the wire to the place where you desire the next bend, until you have created a spiral of the desired width.

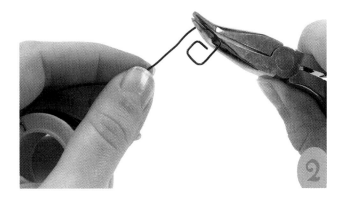

Making Clasps and Hooks

You will be using this basic clasp system for many of the bracelets and necklaces in this book. **Note:** See your chosen project for instructions on cutting wire to a particular length for this process.

Clasp

1 About 2" from the end of a piece of wire, make a large basic anchor loop, wrapping the wire near the base of the round nose pliers.

2 Below the loop, wrap the short end of the wire around the long end of the wire a few times. Cut off any excess.

Hook

1 Bend 2" of a piece of wire over at one end.

2 Use the pliers to wrap the short end around the wire, creating a narrow loop. Cut off any excess.

3 Bend the loop of wire in half.

4 Bend the end of the loop up slightly to create the hook of the clasp.

5 To connect the two pieces of wire, put the hook through the round clasp.

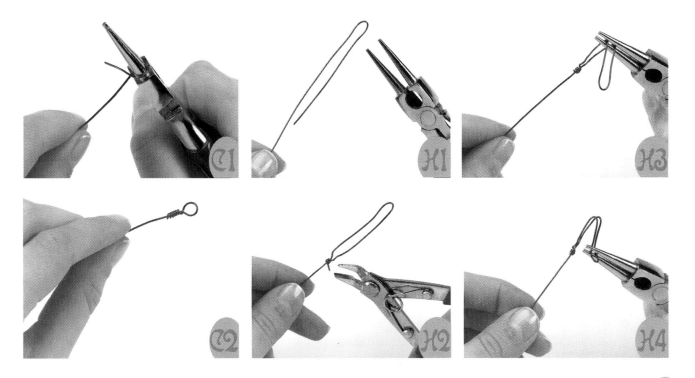

Using the Twist n' Curl to make single, double, and triple coil beads is really quite easy! **Note:** Unless otherwise specified, use the wire as it comes on the spool. Once your coil is complete, you can cut off the excess wire. Instructions for each project in this book will tell you how long to make each coil.

Creating a Coil

This basic coil is also called a single coil bead. You can push the wire together on the rod to make a very tight, compact coil, or pull the ends after you take the coil off of the rod to make a long, loose coil.

1 Screw a rod of any shape or size desired into the hole at the center of the handle.

2 Insert 2" of wire into the wire hole in the handle. Bend the 2" piece of wire so it is flat against the back of the handle.

3 Hold the wire in one hand. As you twist the handle with your other hand, the wire will coil around the rod. Once you have created a coil of the desired length, cut off the excess wire and slip the coil off of the tool.

4 Cut off the excess wire at the beginning of the coil. With round nose pliers, carefully bend the ends of the wire so that they will lie flat with the rest of the coil (the wire is very sharp!).

Here, a single coil becomes a double coil as it is wrapped around the rod and a piece of new wire, which serves as its core.

1 Create a single coil bead as directed on page 12 that is at least 3" long, leaving a 2" piece of straight wire at one end of the coil. Remove the rod.

2 Insert a new piece of wire through the center of the single coil. Attach the end of the new wire into the wire hole in the handle.

3 Wrap the new wire around the rod, creating a new coil.

4 Slide the single coil up to the wrapped wire on the rod. Insert the 2" end of this wire into the hole in the handle.

5 Hold the coil against the rod. As you twist the handle, the single coil will wrap a second time around the rod.

6 At the end of the double coil wrap more of the straight wire around the rod. Cut off the excess wire at both ends of the bead and remove from the rod.

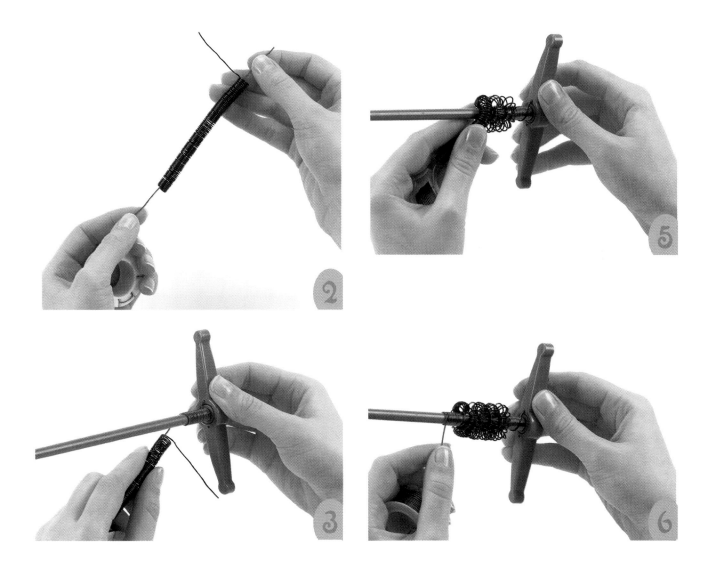

The ultimate wire bead, the triple coil bead uses the same principles as the double coil bead.

1 Create a double coil bead that is at least 6" long, leaving a 2" piece of straight wire at the end of the coil.

2 Insert a new piece of wire through the center of the double coil bead. Attach the end of the new wire into the wire hole in the handle.

3 Wrap the new wire around the rod, creating a new coil.

4 Slide the double coil up to the wrapped wire on the rod. Insert the 2" end of this wire into the hole in the handle.

5 Hold the coil against the rod. As you twist the handle, the double coil will wrap a third time around the rod.

6 At the end of the triple coil wrap more of the straight wire around the rod. Cut off the excess wire at both ends of the bead and remove from the rod.

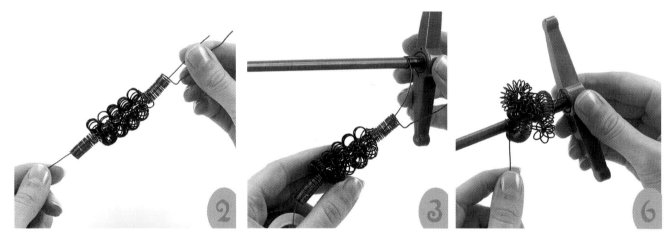

This simple spiral adds the perfect finishing touch to any wire bead you create. This is especially useful for home décor applications.

1 Cut a piece of wire long enough to be threaded through a wire bead or the length desired (if you are just going to string glass beads onto it), allowing excess for an anchor loop at top to connect it to your project.

2 Make a spiral at one end, as directed on page 10.

3 Insert the end of the wire through a wire bead, or slip glass or frosted beads onto it.

4 Now create an anchor loop at the top of the bead.

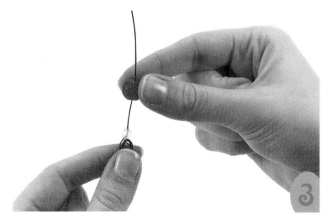

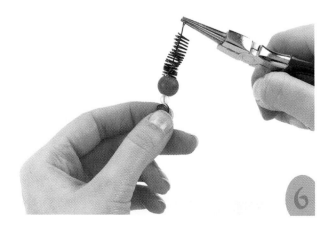

Shaping a basic ear wire is quite easy! Any combination of wire shapes or bead links can then be attached to an ear wire.

1 Cut a 4" piece of wire. Make a loop with round nose pliers, 1" from one end of the wire.

2 Below the loop, wrap the short end of the wire around the long end of the wire a few times. Cut off any excess.

3 Place the jig over the jig pattern, lining up the holes of the jig with the circles on the pattern.

Place a small peg at position A and a large peg at position B.

4 Place the loop formed in Steps 1 and 2 onto peg A. Shape the top curve of the ear wire by wrapping the wire partially around peg B. Let the wire hang straight down on the other side of the peg.

5 Lift the shape off of the jig. Bend the end of the wire up slightly with bent chain nose pliers.

6 Attach the dangling section to the loop formed in Steps 1 and 2.

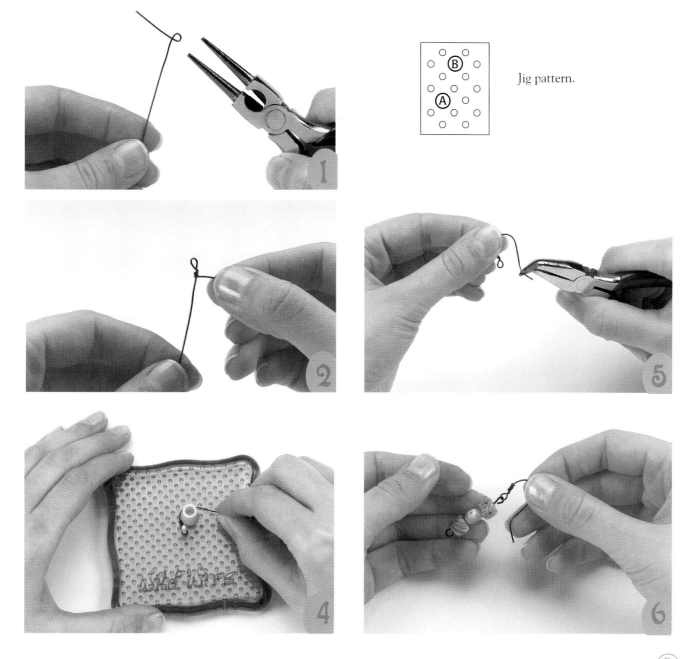

Jig pattern.

A jig is quite easy to use; simply place pegs into the jig as directed in a project's pattern and wrap wire around the pegs to create a shape. There are four different sizes of pegs (small through extra-large); follow the individual project's instructions for which pegs to use.

1 Place the jig over the jig pattern.

2 While looking through the jig, place pegs into it where indicated. Use the size of pegs noted in the project instructions.

3 Make an anchor loop on one end of the wire.

4 Thread the anchor loop onto peg A in the direction shown in the second part of the jig pattern (labeled "wrap directions" in this book), following the arrows.

5 Wrap the wire around the pegs, following the arrow pattern.

6 At the end of the pattern, use wire cutters to snip the wire. Release the pattern from the jig.

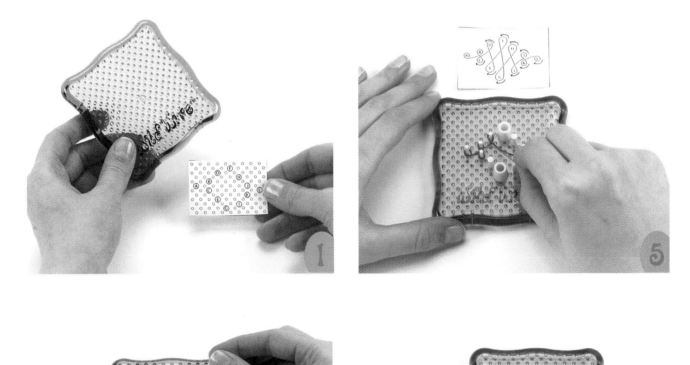

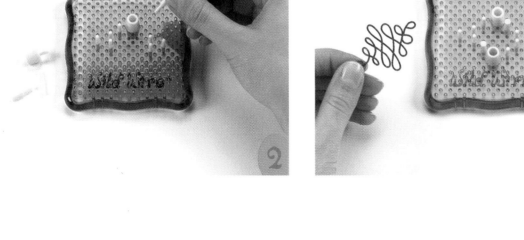

This unique tool allows you to write with wire using a jig. Note that the Wire Writer uses mini-spools of wire, not larger ones.

1 Release one end of the wire from a spool before attaching it to the Wire Writer.

2 Pull the spool lock off of the end of the spool bar. Slide the spool of wire onto the spool bar. Push the spool lock back in place.

3 Guide the free end of wire down through the groove along one side of the Wire Writer. Bring the end of the wire through the nib at the bottom.

4 With your pliers, make an anchor loop in the end of the wire.

5 Place the jig pattern under the jig and insert the pegs, as directed in the project instructions.

6 Slip the anchor loop around peg A and use the Wire Writer to follow the jig pattern.

7 At the end of the pattern, use wire cutters to snip the wire. Release the pattern from the jig.

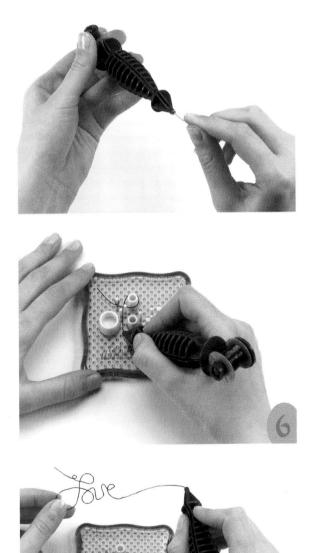

Be-Dazzler

Supplies and Basic Techniques

The Original Be-Dazzler Stud and Rhinestone Setting Machine™ has been used to create fashionable projects for more than two decades—the following pages will introduce you to the basics of working with this tool, as well as other products in the Be-Dazzler family.

A variety of studs.

The Original Be-Dazzler Stud and Rhinestone Setting Machine.

Supplies

The Be-Dazzler Machine safely and accurately sets studs into fabric. It adjusts easily to fit the round studs in the Be-Dazzler range and can also set rhinestones with a tiffany setting. The Stud Insertion Tool is a must! This tool is included in the Be-Dazzler Stud and Rhinestone Setting Machine Set. This tool safely inserts studs and settings into the Be-Dazzler machine, without your fingers having to press down on the sharp points of the prongs.

Be-Dazzler gold- and silver-colored studs come in many different sizes and shapes. Each stud has a decorative front with sharp prongs on the back to secure the stud to the fabric. Colorful rhinestones can also be attached to fabric. A tiffany style setting with prongs is required to set rhinestones.

The Be-Dazzler Custom Hand Tool sets very large or unusually shaped studs, including hearts, horseshoes, and peace signs, into fabric. This tool is also very helpful for the paper applications in this book.

Custom Hand Tool.

The Be-Dazzler machine can set #20, #34, #40, and #60 round studs and rhinestones. This includes all flathead studs, round diamond cut studs, pearl studs, ringlets, mirrors, small flowers, small stars, and happy face studs. Two parts of the Be-Dazzler machine have to be changed each time you set a new size stud: the plunger and the setter plate.

Changing the Plunger

The Be-Dazzler machine comes with four different sized plungers. Choose the plunger that matches the size of the stud or rhinestone you are setting (for example, a #20 plunger would be used to set #20 studs).

1 To insert the correct size plunger, lift the arm of the Be-Dazzler and slide the plunger holder down and out of the arm.

2 Pull apart the two halves of the plunger holder and remove the plunger. To insert another plunger, fit one tab at the top of the plunger into the notch on one half of the plunger holder. Close the two halves of the holder.

3 To slide the plunger holder back into the arm of the machine, fit the long tab along one side of the holder into the long groove inside the opening of the arm.

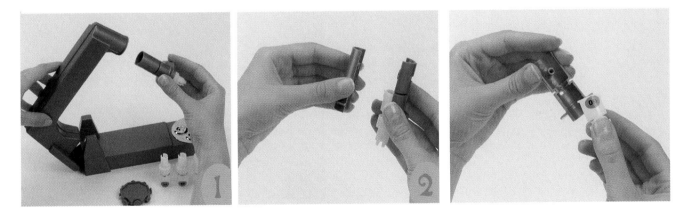

Adjusting the Setter Plate

The setter plate, located on the base of the machine, has four settings. **Note:** If the setter plate does not turn easily, the plate can be adjusted. Use a Phillips screwdriver to loosen the screw at the center of the plate. Turn the wing nut (located at the other end of the screw, under the machine) as you loosen or tighten the screw.

1 Rotate the setter plate according to the size of your stud. If you are setting a #20 stud, for example, turn the setter plate so that the tip of the plunger aims directly down into the center of the #20 setting.

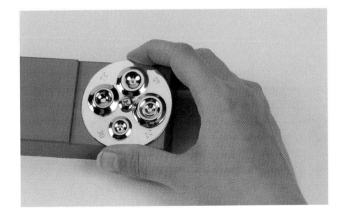

Always use the insertion tool to insert studs into the Be-Dazzler machine! The sides of the tool correspond to the different size studs or rhinestone settings. There are two types of tips for each size: a flat tip and a pointed tip. Use the flat tip for studs and the pointed tip for rhinestone tiffany settings.

1 To set a stud, slip a #60 stud over the #60, for example, onto the flat tip of the tool. With the stud held in place on the insertion tool, push the stud securely into the tip of the plunger.

2 Place your fabric, right side up, over the setter plate on the machine. Lower the arm of the machine, checking for accurate placement of the stud, then press firmly on the arm to set the stud into the fabric.

3 After each stud is inserted, check the back of the fabric. Each prong of the stud should be bent in toward the center, and all of the prongs should lie flat against the fabric and not stick out. If any prongs do stick out, use the tip of the insertion tool or the Custom Hand Tool to flatten them. If the prongs are facing the wrong direction, the setter plate is probably not centered under the plunger tip; also, make sure to use the correct setter plate.

Setting Rhinestones

As was mentioned previously, you will use the pointed side of the insertion tool to set rhinestones onto your project.

1 Rhinestones are held onto the fabric with a tiffany setting. Slip a tiffany setting onto the pointed tip of the insertion tool. Use the insertion tool to push the setting into the plunger in the arm of the machine.

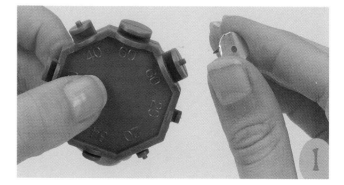

2 Place a rhinestone upside down in the setter plate.

3 Place your fabric right side down over the setter plate. (**Note:** When setting rhinestones, it might be helpful to mark your design on the wrong side of the fabric with a vanishing or washable fabric mark-er). Lower the arm of the machine, checking for accurate placement, then press firmly on the arm to insert the tiffany setting. If inserted correctly, the prongs of the setting will go through to the front of the fabric and bend securely around the rhinestone.

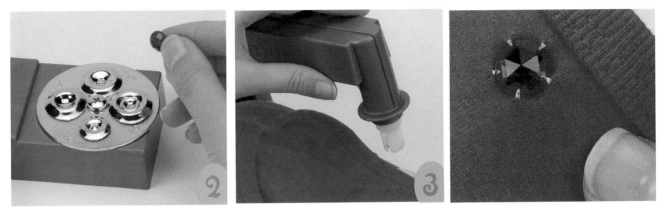

Directions for Using the Be-Dazzler Custom Hand Tool

Very large or unusually shaped studs can be inserted into fabric with the Custom Hand Tool. Follow this process for adding studs to any of the paper-related projects in this book.

1 Position the stud on the right side of the fabric. With your fingers, carefully press the stud's prongs through the fabric.

2 Turn the fabric to the back and check that each prong came through the fabric all of the way. You may need to press the fabric around each prong to ensure a tight fit. Avoid touching the tips of the prongs.

3 Slip one prong of the stud inside the small slit on the hand tool. Use the tool to bend the prong in toward the center. Once all of the prongs are bent in toward the center, use the raised rounded area of the tool to press them flat against the fabric.

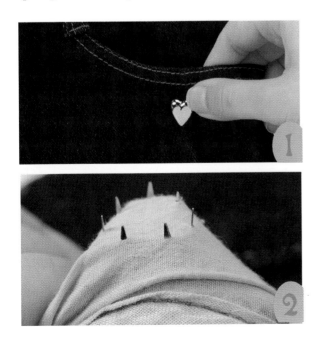

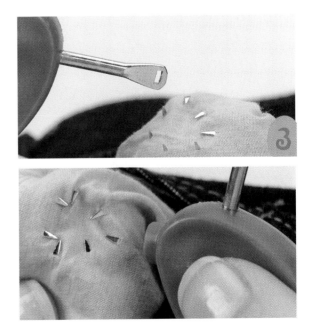

Section 1
Projects for You

Using wire to make unique pieces of jewelry to match your wardrobe may seem like a daunting task, but fear not! If you practice using the tools and trying the basic techniques presented earlier in this book, you will not have any difficulty creating beautiful necklaces, earrings, bracelets, and even unexpected items, like rings and hair accessories. Let the projects in this section serve as inspiration—by choosing your own combinations of wire colors and gauges, as well as various types of glass and pony beads, you will open the doors to creativity and exploration and make pieces that will be the envy of friends and family.

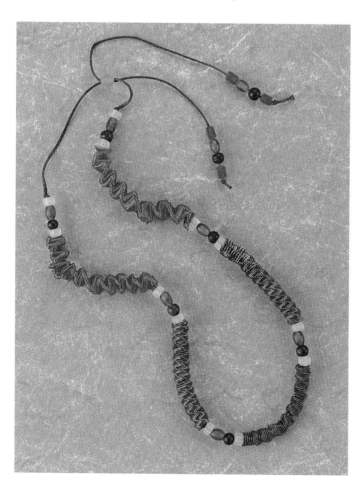 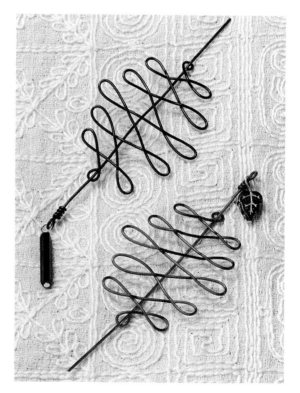

Red, White, and Blue Necklace

Show your patriotism throughout the year with this stunning double coil and bead necklace.

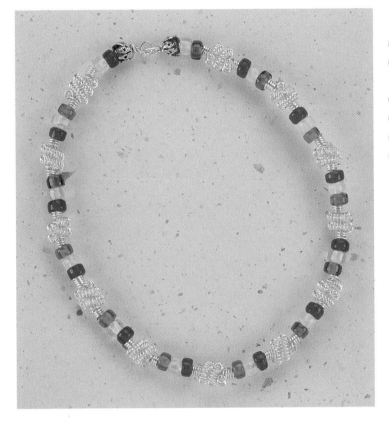

You Will Need

- 22 gauge wire, Bare (silver)
- 39 pony beads (13 of each color), 1/4" wide red, clear, blue
- 2 decorative jewelry findings, silver
- Round Nose Pliers
- Twist n' Curl and small metal rod
- Wire Cutter

1 With the Twist n' Curl, make 12 double coil beads; both the core and outer bead will be made from bare (silver) wire. Each completed bead should be approximately 3/4" long.

2 Cut one 20" piece of wire. At one end, make a clasp.

3 String one of the decorative findings onto the wire. Wrap wire around the finding, securing it in place.

4 String three pony beads onto the wire, alternating red, clear, and blue. After the three pony beads, string on one double coil bead. Continue stringing pony beads and wire beads onto the wire, alternating them in this fashion.

5 After all of the beads are strung, put on the final finding; wrap wire around it to secure.

6 With the remaining wire, make a hook.

Heart Pendant Necklace

This coiled and spiraled necklace has a unique heart-shaped pendant that is accented with a large glass bead.

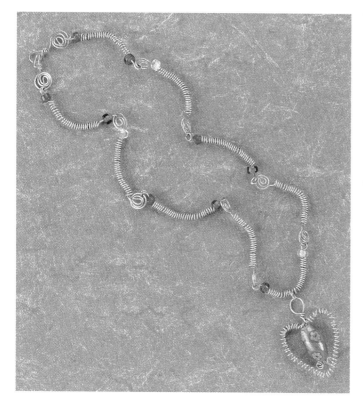

You Will Need

- 18 gauge wire, Bare (silver)
- 10 to 18 pony beads, 1/4" wide, various colors
- 1 large glass bead
- Twist n' Curl and small metal rod
- Round Nose Pliers
- Nylon Jaw Pliers
- Wire Cutter

1 Using the Twist n' Curl, make five coiled beads. Leave enough wire at each end to slip on a pony bead and make an anchor loop. Each resulting bead should be about 2-1/2" long.

2 Make four additional coiled beads, but this time leave enough wire at each end to create a 1/2" wide spiral. **Optional:** Slip a pony bead onto each end of the wire prior to making the spiral.

3 Bend the coiled beads make in Steps 1 and 2 slightly to shape and curve them.

4 To assemble the necklace, join a coiled bead with anchor loops onto a spiraled bead. Continue alternating coiled beads until you have joined all nine.

5 Coil another piece of wire, leaving about 1-1/2" uncoiled at each end; the coil should be 4" long. Shape the coil into a heart, brining the uncoiled ends to the middle. Slip the large glass bead onto the two uncoiled ends and make an anchor loop in each end to hold the bead into place.

6 Cut a 1-1/2" piece of wire. Make a large loop in the wire, directly in the middle, using the base of the round nose pliers. Curl the ends of this loop around the heart pendant, near the top.

7 Make one wire jump ring and attach the heart pendant to the middle coil of the necklace.

8 Using two different pieces of wire, make a small clasp and a small hook, leaving enough excess wire to make a spiral. With the remaining ends of wire, make a spiral. Attach the spiraled end of the clasp to the anchor loop of one coiled bead. Attach the hook to the coiled bead on the other end of the necklace.

3 Beaded Blue Barrette

This pretty blue barrette is attached to a standard clasp barrette, so there are no chances of your hair getting tangled in the wire!

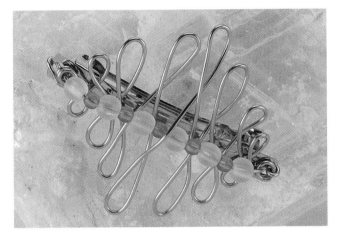

You Will Need

- 18 gauge wire, Light Blue
- 11 frosted glass beads, 3/16" to 1/4" wide, blue and white
- 1 barrette, 2-1/2" long, silver
- Jig and pegs
- Round Nose Pliers
- Wire Cutter

1 Place the jig over the jig pattern, lining up the holes of the jig with the circles on the pattern. Place small pegs at A, B, C, D, E, L, M, N, O, and P and medium pegs at F, G, H, I, J, and K.

2 Make an anchor loop on one end of the wire and slip it onto peg A; follow the design. After completing the design, set aside.

3 Cut a piece of wire that is 4" long. Thread the beads onto the wire, alternating blue and white.

4 Set the jigged design made in Step 1 on the barrette, lining up the holes in the barrette ends with the looped ends of the design. Carefully thread the piece of wire with the beads through the end loop of the jigged design and the hole in one end of the barrette. Wrap this wire tightly to secure; cut off any excess.

5 Slip the beaded wire under the longest part of the jigged design.

6 Thread the remaining end of the beaded wire through the other end loop and barrette hole. Wrap as in Step 3.

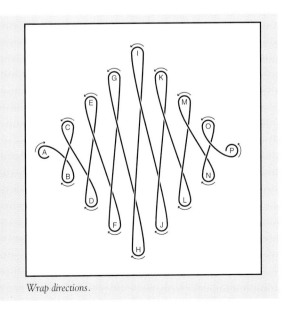

Jig pattern.

Wrap directions.

Project 4

Double Coil Set

This summery colored set is made with double coil beads. The necklace adds one triple coil bead, which is the focal point.

You Will Need

- 24 gauge wire, Bare (silver), Light Blue, Dark Blue
- 32 round beads, 1/8" wide, blue and silver
- Twist n' Curl and small metal rod
- Wire Cutter

Necklace

1 Make 14 double coil beads. Begin each with a single coil that is 3" long. With the color of wire you want to use for the clasp, complete each double coil bead, making a 1/4" coil at each end of the bead. (If you want to alternate colors of beads as shown in the sample, make seven of one color and seven of another.)

2 Make one triple coil bead. Begin the triple coil with a single coil that is 9" long. To make a coil that is longer than the length of the rod, see page 45.

3 Cut a 22" piece of wire; make a hook at one end.

4 String three round beads and a double coil bead onto the wire. Continue to alternate beads with the double coil beads until there are seven double coil beads on the wire. After the last set of beads, add the triple coil bead. Continue alternating double coil beads and beads to complete the necklace.

5 Make a clasp with the remaining end of wire.

Bracelet

See the instructions for the Double Coil Bracelet on the following page to make the bracelet for this set. Note that those instructions ask for five beads that are each 3" long, whereas here you will need eight beads that are each approximately 1" long.

Earrings

1 Make two ear wires; make an anchor loop at the bottom.

2 Create two double coil beads, each with two beads as the "drop," and attach them to the ear wires.

5 Double Coil Bracelet

Here's another opportunity to practice making double coil beads!

You Will Need

- 24 and 26 gauge wire, Dark Green, Tinned Copper, Violet, Green, Black
- 6 round beads, 1/8" wide, copper
- Twist n' Curl and small metal rod
- Wire Cutter

1 Make five double coil beads. Begin each double coil with a single coil that is 3" long. With the same color wire used for the single coil, complete each double coil bead, making a 1/4" coil at each end of the bead.

2 Measure and cut an 11" piece of wire. This piece of wire will be used to make the clasp system of the bracelet.

3 Make a hook on one end of the wire.

4 String a round bead onto the wire. Next string a double coil bead and then another round bead onto the wire. Continue to alternate beads, stringing all five double coil beads onto the wire. End with a round bead.

5 Make a clasp with the remaining end of wire.

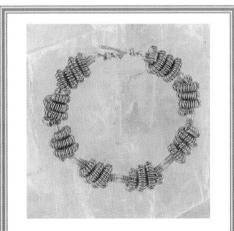

This bracelet has eight shorter double coil beads, all made with the same pretty light blue and silver wire. The clear glass beads add a classy touch.

Project 6

Drop Necklace

This delicate necklace has a pretty "drop" that encloses three beads.

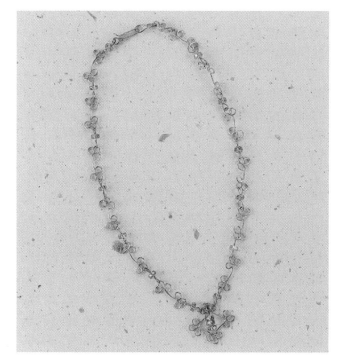

You Will Need

- 22 gauge wire, Gold
- 17 glass beads, 1/4" wide, blue
- Jig and pegs
- Round Nose Pliers
- Wire Cutter

make an anchor loop with the remaining wire. Use this top anchor loop to attach the "drop" to the jigged design made in Step 5.

7 To assemble the necklace, start with one bead link and connect a jigged design from Step 2 to it. Continue alternating bead links and jigged designs until you have used seven bead links. At this point, attach the completed "drop" from Step 6 to the bead link. After this piece is connected, continue alternating bead links and jigged designs.

8 Using two different pieces of wire, make a clasp and a hook. Attach the clasp to a bead link on one end of the necklace and the hook to the other end.

1 Place the jig over jig pattern A, lining up the holes of the jig with the circles on the pattern. Place a small peg at each position.

2 Make an anchor loop in the end of the wire. Slip the anchor loop onto peg A and follow the design. Twist the wire tightly around peg F, cut the excess wire, and remove from the jig. Repeat this process to make 12 jigged designs.

3 Cut a 1" piece of wire. Make a bead link with this piece of wire and one blue bead. Make 14 bead links in this manner.

4 Place the jig over jig pattern B, lining up the holes of the jig with the circles on the pattern. Place a small peg at each position.

5 Make an anchor loop in the end of the wire. Slip the anchor loop onto peg A and follow the design. Make a double loop around peg A after you have completed the design. Cut the excess wire and remove from the jig.

6 Cut a 1" piece of wire. Make a very small anchor loop on one end. Slide on three blue beads and

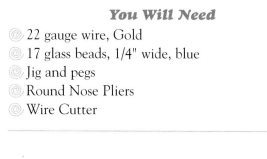

Jig pattern A.

Wrap directions A.

Jig pattern B.

Wrap directions B.

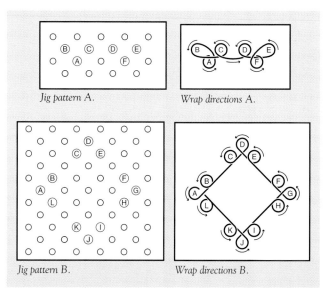

 Gold Filigree Necklace

This dainty necklace combines pretty jigged designs and simple bead links.

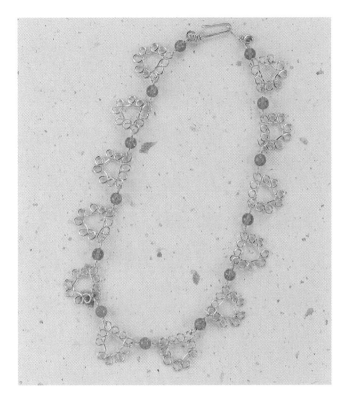

You Will Need

- 22 gauge wire, Gold
- 13 round beads, 1/4" wide, blue
- Jig and pegs
- Round Nose Pliers
- Wire Cutter

1 Place the jig over the jig pattern, lining up the holes of the jig with the circles on the pattern. Place a small peg at each position.

2 Make an anchor loop in the end of the wire. Slip the anchor loop onto peg A and follow the design. Twist the wire tightly around peg J, cut the excess wire, and remove from the jig. Repeat this process to make 12 jigged designs.

3 Cut a 1" piece of wire. Make a bead link with this piece of wire and one blue bead. Make 13 bead links in this manner.

4 To assemble the necklace, start with one bead link and connect a jigged design from Step 2 to it. Continue alternating bead links and jigged designs until you have used all of the components.

5 Using two different pieces of wire, make a clasp and a hook. Attach the clasp to a bead link on one of the necklace and the hook to the other end.

Jig pattern.

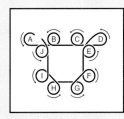

Wrap directions.

Triangular Bead Necklace

This fun necklace uses both triangular and teardrop shaped beads that create interesting lines when combined with jigged designs.

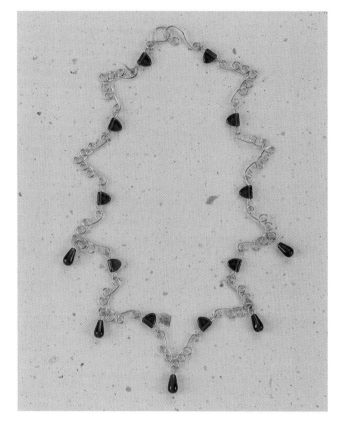

You Will Need

- 22 gauge wire, Gold
- 10 triangular beads, 5mm wide, blue
- 5 teardrop shaped beads, 6mm long, blue
- Jig and pegs
- Round Nose Pliers
- Wire Cutter

5 Cut a 1" piece of wire. Make a small anchor loop in one end. Slip on a teardrop shaped bead and make an anchor loop in the remaining end.

6 Find the middle of the necklace (the fifth jigged design); attach a bead from Step 5 onto the lowest point of this jigged design. Attach the four remaining beads to the two jigged designs on either side of this central design.

7 Using two different pieces of wire, make a clasp and a hook. The hook shown here is rounded; make one anchor loop, curve the wire to resemble an ear wire and make a final anchor loop. Attach the clasp to a bead link on one of the necklace and the hook to the other end.

1 Place the jig over the jig pattern, lining up the holes of the jig with the circles on the pattern. Place a small peg at each position.

2 Make an anchor loop in the end of the wire. Slip the anchor loop onto peg A and follow the design. Twist the wire tightly around peg G, cut the excess wire, and remove from the jig. Repeat this process to make nine jigged designs.

3 Cut a 1" piece of wire. Make a bead link with this piece of wire and one triangular bead. Make 10 bead links in this manner.

4 To assemble the necklace, start with one bead link and connect a jigged design from Step 2 to it. Continue alternating bead links and jigged designs until you have used all of the components.

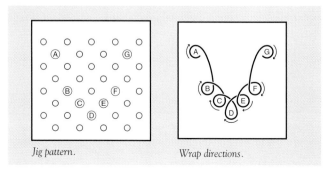

Jig pattern.   Wrap directions.

Linked Necklace

Glass beads are the focal point of this classy necklace.

You Will Need

- 22 gauge wire, Gold
- 10 glass beads, 5mm wide, blue
- Jig and pegs
- Round Nose Pliers
- Wire Cutter

1 Place the jig over the jig pattern, lining up the holes of the jig with the circles on the pattern. Place a small peg at A and C and a large peg at B.

2 Make an anchor loop in the end of the wire. Slip the anchor loop onto peg A and follow the design. Twist the wire tightly around peg C and back up to A, cut the excess wire, and remove from the jig. Repeat this process to make nine jigged designs.

3 Cut a 1-1/2" piece of wire. Make a bead link with this piece of wire and one blue bead, coiling the wire on either side of the bead. Make 10 bead links in this manner.

4 To assemble the necklace, start with one bead link and connect a jigged design from Step 2 to it. Continue alternating bead links and jigged designs until you have used all of the components.

5 Using two different pieces of wire, make a clasp and a hook. Attach the clasp to a bead link on one of the necklace and the hook to the other end.

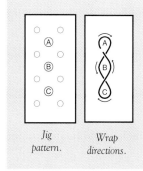

Jig
pattern.

Wrap
directions.

Bare Copper Tri-Level Bracelet

This bracelet is a little complicated to make, but the results are stunning! We have shown it in both copper and gold with the same delicate blue beads, so the choice is yours!

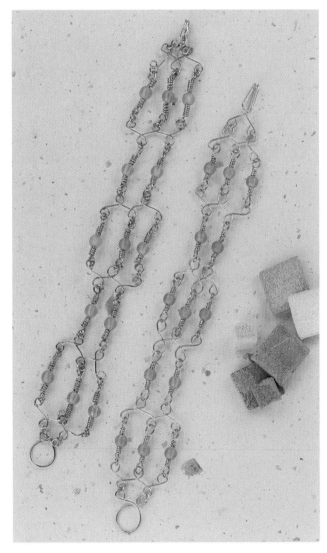

You Will Need

- 20 gauge wire, Copper or Gold
- 13 beads, 5mm wide, blue
- Jig and pegs
- Round Nose Pliers
- Bent Chain Nose Pliers
- Wire Cutter

cedure twelve more times for a total of 13 bead links.

4 Place the jig over jig pattern A, lining up the holes of the jig with the circles on the pattern. Place a small peg at each position.

5 Cut a 5" piece of wire and create an anchor loop at one end of the wire.

6 Slip the anchor loop onto peg A. Bring the wire around peg B with your fingers. As you do this, loop the wire tightly around, pushing it down to the base of the peg.

7 As you wrap the wire around peg C, slip the loop of one bead link (made in Steps 1 to 3) on the wire. Complete the shape by wrapping the wire around pegs D and E. Lift the shape with its attached bead link off of the jig and cut off the excess wire.

8 Open the loops that were formed at pegs A and E with bent chain nose pliers and hook a bead link at each loop. Re-tighten the loops.

9 Keeping the five small pegs in the same formation, cut another 5" piece of wire and make an anchor loop at one end. Slip the anchor loop onto peg A. As you bring the wire around peg B, slide another bead link onto the wire.

10 As you bring the wire around peg C, turn the shape with its attached bead links (completed in Step 8) around so that the middle bead link of that shape can slide onto the wire of this new shape. The two wire shapes should now be connected by the bead link at peg C.

1 To create a bead link, measure 1" from the end of a piece of wire and create an eye loop with round nose pliers at this point.

2 Below the loop, wrap the short end of the wire around the long end of the wire. Slide a bead onto the wire.

3 After the bead, create another loop, leaving a small space between the bead and the loop for you to wrap the end of the wire around. Repeat this entire pro-

11 Slip another bead link onto the wire and wrap the wire around peg D. Complete the shape by wrapping the wire around peg E. Lift the shape off of the jig and cut off the excess wire. Twist open the loops of the new wire shape that were formed at pegs A and E. Attach the other two bead links from the original wire shape to these opened loops. Twist the loops closed.

12 Again, keep the five pegs in the same formation on the jig and cut another 5" piece of wire. Make an anchor loop at one end. Slip the anchor loop onto peg A.

13 Turn the completed part of the bracelet around so that the attached two bead links face pegs B and D on the jig. As you wrap the wire around peg B, bring the wire through the loop of the nearest bead link.

14 As you wrap the wire around peg C, slide on a new bead link. As you wrap the wire around peg D, bring the wire through the other bead link of the bracelet. Complete this shape by wrapping the wire around peg E. Twist open the loops of the new wire shape that were formed at pegs A and E and hook a bead link on each loop. Tighten the loops again.

15 Repeat Steps 9 to 14 one more time. At this point you should have all 13 bead links attached to the bracelet.

16 Cut another 5" piece of wire and create an anchor loop at the end. Keeping the same five pegs on the jig, slip the loop onto peg A, then bring the wire around peg B. Bring the wire through the middle bead link of the bracelet and wrap the wire around peg C. Complete the shape by wrapping the

wire around peg D and peg E. Lift the shape off of the jig and cut off the excess wire. Attach the last two hanging bead links to the loops formed at pegs A and E.

17 To create the clasp, lay the jig over jig pattern B. Place a small peg at positions A and C. Place a large peg at position B.

18 Cut a 4" piece of wire and create an anchor loop at one end. Slip the anchor loop onto peg A. Wrap the wire around peg B. Complete the shape by wrapping the wire around peg C. Lift the shape off of the jig, cut off the excess wire, and tighten the final loop.

19 To create the hook, lay the jig over jig pattern C. Place a small peg at positions A and C and a large peg at B. Cut a 6" piece of wire and create an anchor loop at one end.

20 Slip the anchor loop onto peg A. Bring the wire around peg B, then complete the shape by circling around peg C. Lift the shape off the jig, cut off the excess wire and tighten the final loop.

21 Use round nose pliers to bend the long loop of the shape in half. Then bend the looped end up.

22 With the excess wire, create four wire jump rings.

23 To attach the clasp, twist open two of the jump rings and hook the rings onto the two small loops of the clasp and onto the outer two loops of the bracelet. Twist the rings closed. Repeat at the other end, attaching the hook to the bracelet with the remaining two jump rings.

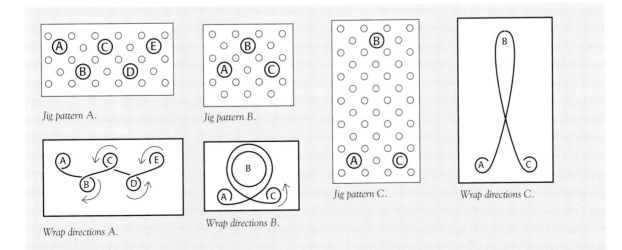

Jig pattern A.

Jig pattern B.

Jig pattern C.

Wrap directions A.

Wrap directions B.

Wrap directions C.

Coiled Bead Set

Designed by Elaine Schmidt

You are sure to have fun experimenting with wire of different colors with this coiled set.

You Will Need
- 22 gauge wire, Powder Blue
- 24 gauge wire, Violet, Turquoise, Tinned Copper, Black
- 21 frosted glass beads, floral designs, in various colors and sizes
- Twist n' Curl and various rods
- Round Nose Pliers
- Wire Cutter

Necklace

1. Make 16 single coils, each 1" long, with the Twist n' Curl, small metal rod, and black wire.

2. Remove the small metal rod from the tool and screw in the largest flat bar. Wrap wire around the flat bar, making a 1/2" long coil. When you remove the coil from the tool, notice how the coil twists, creating a new shape. Try out the other large bars, including the triangle and square bars, to create interesting shapes. Make a total of 16 large coils of different colors.

3. Cut a 22" piece of wire and make a hook at the end.

4. Make one long continuous strand of coils by slipping all of the black coils made in Step 1 onto the wire.

5. Slide one of the larger coils over the strand, covering the smaller coils underneath. Slide the large coil down to the hook. Slide a bead over the strand, then add another large coil. Continue to alternate glass beads and large coils, covering the entire strand of small coils.

6. Make a clasp with the remaining piece of the wire.

Bracelet

Make this bracelet following the instructions for the necklace, except make four wire beads and use five glass beads.

Ring

1 Make a single coil with powder blue wire that is 2" to 3" long.

2 Cut a piece of black wire that is 6" long; slip the blue wire from Step 1 onto this wire. Run each end of the black wire through a glass bead.

3 Wrap the wire ends on either side of the glass bead; cut off excess wire.

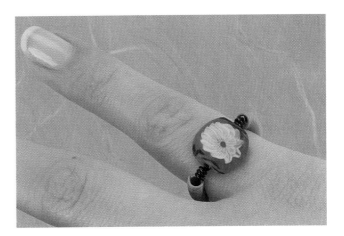

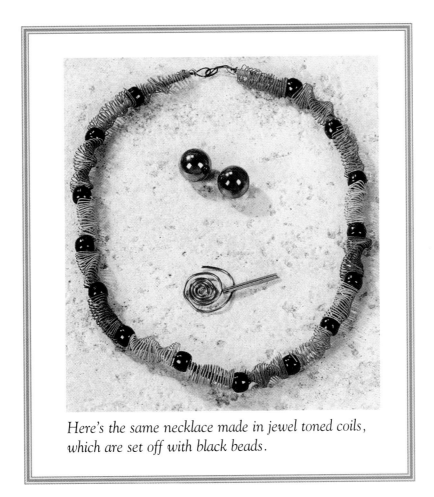

Here's the same necklace made in jewel toned coils, which are set off with black beads.

gewel-tone gewelry get

Designed by Elaine Schmidt

The bracelet shown here is a variation of that shown on page 27, and the accompanying pin and ring can be made in virtually no time at all!

You Will Need
◎ 26 gauge wire, Plum, Peacock Blue
◎ 24 gauge wire, Black
◎ 18 gauge wire, Copper
◎ 6 frosted glass beads, 3mm wide, black
◎ Jig and pegs
◎ Twist n' Curl and small metal rod
◎ Round Nose Pliers
◎ Nylon Jaw Pliers
◎ File
◎ Wire Cutter

Bracelet
Follow the instructions on page 27 to make this bracelet. Use black wire for the core of the double coil beads, purple and blue wire for the double coils, and the copper wire as the center of the bracelet, which makes up the hook and clasp. Use black frosted beads between the double coils

Pin
1 Place the jig over the jig pattern, lining up the holes of the jig with the circles on the pattern. Place a small peg at each position.

2 Make an anchor loop at one end of the copper wire. Slip the anchor loop onto peg A. Follow the jig pattern, making a double wrap at pegs A and K for extra stability.

3 Cut the wire about 3" from the double ending loop. Bend the starting and ending loops 90 degrees, toward the back of the pin. Open the beginning bottom loop to form the hook. File the wire tail into a sharp point for the pin.

4 Create three double coil beads, two blue and one purple, each about 1" long. Make three eye pins with copper wire; create a spiral on one end. Slip each bead onto a spiraled eye pin.

5 Open the top loop of each spiraled eye pin and attach the three beads to the pin; attach the purple bead to the central turn, and the two blue beads to the outermost turns.

Ring
1 Make a single coil with blue wire that is long enough to fit around your finger.

2 Slip the coil onto a 5" to 6" long piece of copper wire. Spiral each end of the wire.

3 Bend the wire into a ring shape and interlock the spirals.

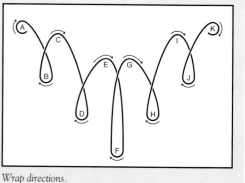

Jig pattern.   Wrap directions.

13 Gold and Pink Drop Necklace

Rectangular beads add a sophisticated feel to this necklace.

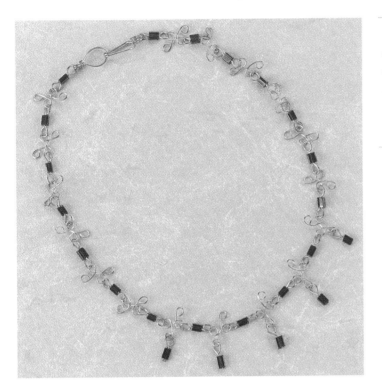

You Will Need

- 22 gauge wire, Gold
- 23 rectangular beads, 3mm wide, pink
- Jig and pegs
- Round Nose Pliers
- Wire Cutter

1 Place the jig over the jig pattern, lining up the holes of the jig with the circles on the pattern. Place a small peg at each position.

2 Make an anchor loop in the end of the wire. Slip the anchor loop onto peg A and follow the design. Twist the wire tightly around peg D, cut the excess wire, and remove from the jig. Repeat this process to make 17 jigged designs.

3 Cut a 3/4" piece of wire. Make a bead link with this piece of wire and one rectangular bead. Make 18 bead links in this manner.

4 To assemble the necklace, start with one bead link and connect a jigged design from Step 2 to it. Continue alternating bead links and jigged designs until you have used all of the components.

5 Cut a 3/4" piece of wire. Make a small anchor loop in one end. Slip on a bead and make an anchor loop in the remaining end. Repeat this produce four additional times to make a total of five "drop" beads.

6 Find the middle of the necklace (the ninth jigged design); attach a bead from Step 5 onto the lowest point of this jigged design. Attach the four remaining beads to the two jigged designs on either side of this central design.

7 Using two different pieces of wire, make a clasp and a hook. Attach the clasp to a bead link on one of the necklace and the hook to the other end.

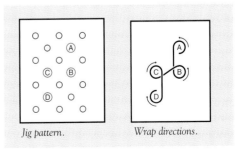

Jig pattern.   Wrap directions.

Tinned Copper Double-banded Bracelet

You will use simple jump rings to connect the various pieces of this pretty bracelet.

You Will Need

- 20 gauge wire, Copper
- 42 beads, 5mm wide, purple
- Jig and pegs
- Round Nose Pliers
- Wire Cutter

6 Add three more beads onto the wire, then wrap the wire around pegs G and H. Complete the shape by winding the wire around peg A again.

7 Lift the shape off of the jig and cut off the excess wire. Tighten the final loop. **Note:** The two loops that circled around peg A will tend to separate once the shape has been lifted off of the jig. When the shape is connected to the other shapes of the bracelet, the two loops will stay together. Repeat Steps 1 to 7 six more times, creating seven identical shapes for the bracelet.

8 To create the clasp, lay the jig over jig pattern B. Place a small peg at positions A and C. Place a large peg at position B.

9 Cut a 3" piece of wire and create an anchor loop at one end. Slip the anchor loop onto peg A. Wrap the wire around peg B. Complete the shape by wrapping the wire around peg C. Lift the shape off of the jig, cut off the excess wire, and tighten the final loop.

10 To create the hook, lay the jig over jig pattern C. Place a small peg at all three positions. Cut a 6" piece of wire and create an anchor loop at one end.

1 Place the jig over jig pattern A, lining up the holes of the jig with the circles on the pattern. Place a small peg at each position.

2 Cut an 8" piece of wire and create an anchor loop at one end.

3 Slip the anchor loop onto peg A. Bring the wire around peg B with your fingers. As you do this, loop the wire tightly around, pushing it down to the base of the peg.

4 Slide three beads on the straight end of the wire, pushing the beads up against peg B.

5 Loop the wire tightly around pegs C and D. Continue by looping the wire around peg E, then peg F.

11 Slip the anchor loop onto peg A. Bring the wire around peg B, then complete the shape by circling around peg C. Lift the shape off of the jig, cut off the excess wire, and tighten the final loop.

12 Use round nose pliers to bend the long loop of the shape in half. Then bend the looped end up.

13 With the excess wire, create 16 wire jump rings.

14 To assemble the bracelet, twist open two of the jump rings and hook the rings onto the two small loops of the clasp. Hook one bead link onto each jump ring as well, then squeeze the jump rings closed. Continue to attach each bead link with jump rings until all of the links are attached. Complete the bracelet by attaching the hook onto the last bead link with jump rings.

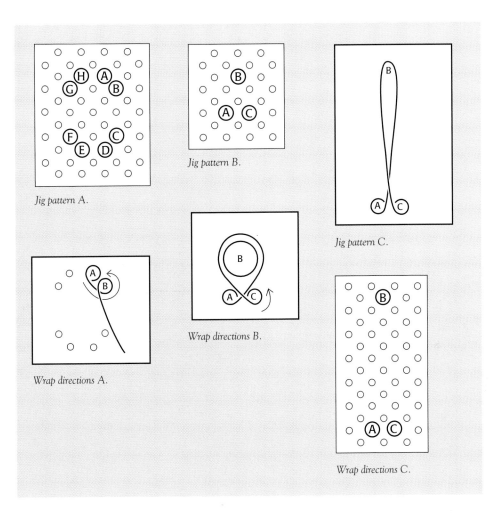

Jig pattern A.

Jig pattern B.

Jig pattern C.

Wrap directions A.

Wrap directions B.

Wrap directions C.

Twisted Loop Set

Twisted and turned wire in a bright color will add lots of pizzazz to your wardrobe! For a one-of-a-kind look, try hand-twisting two pieces of wire together for all of the jigged shapes.

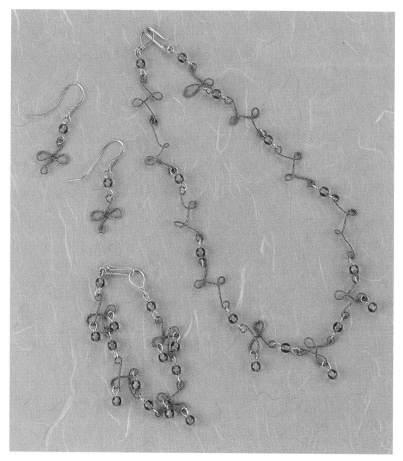

You Will Need

- 26 gauge wire, Plum
- 20 round beads, 3/8" wide, purple
- Jig and pegs
- Round Nose Pliers
- Wire Cutter

final loop. Repeat Steps 1 to 4 an additional 10 times for a total of 11 wire shapes.

5 Cut a 2" piece of wire, make an anchor loop at one end, slide on one bead, and make a final loop after the bead. Repeat until you have a total of 15 bead links.

6 Cut a piece of wire and create a clasp. Cut a piece of wire and create a hook.

7 To assemble the necklace, twist open one loop of a bead link and attach it to the small loops of the clasp. Twist the loop closed again. Attach a wire shape to the bead link. Continue alternating bead links and wire shapes until you have made a chain of 11 wire shapes and 12 bead links. Attach the hook to the last bead link.

8 You have three remaining bead links. Add one to the center three wire shapes of the necklace.

Necklace

1 Place the jig over the jig pattern, lining up the holes of the jig with the circles on the pattern. Place a small peg at positions A and D. Place a medium peg at positions B and C.

2 Cut a 4" piece of wire and create an anchor loop at one end of the wire.

3 Slip the anchor loop onto peg A. Bring the wire around peg B with your fingers. As you do this, loop the wire tightly around, pushing it down to the base of the peg.

4 Wrap the wire around peg C. Complete the shape by wrapping the wire around peg D. Lift the shape off the jig and cut off the excess wire. Tighten the

Bracelet

1 Follow Steps 1 to 6 of the necklace instructions, making four wire shapes, 13 bead links, and both a clasp and a hook.

2 To assemble the bracelet, twist open one loop of a bead link and attach it to the small loops of the clasp. Twist the loop closed again. Attach a wire shape to the bead link. Continue alternating bead links and wire shapes until you have made a chain of

four wire shapes and five bead links. Attach the hook to the last bead link.

3 You have eight remaining bead links. Add two bead links to each of the wire shapes of the bracelet.

Earrings

1 Follow Steps 1 to 5 of the necklace instructions, making one wire shape and one bead link for each earring.

2 Make one ear wire for each earring.

3 To assemble the earrings, twist open one loop of a bead link and attach it to the loop of the ear wire. Twist the loop closed again. Attach a wire shape to the other end of the bead link.

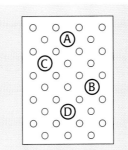

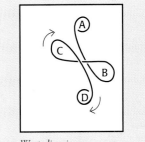

Jig pattern.   Wrap directions.

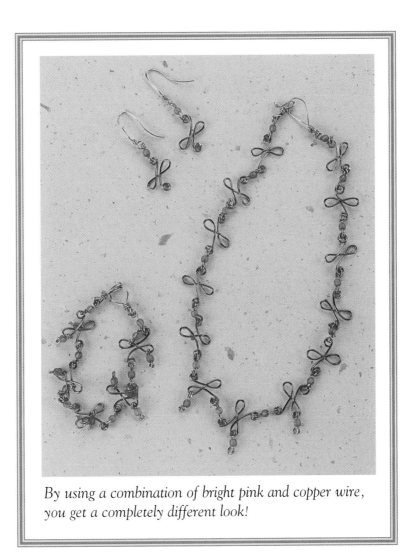

By using a combination of bright pink and copper wire, you get a completely different look!

16 Beaded Barrettes

Designed by Lauren Johnston

These elegant barrettes incorporate different sized glass beads strung onto wire.

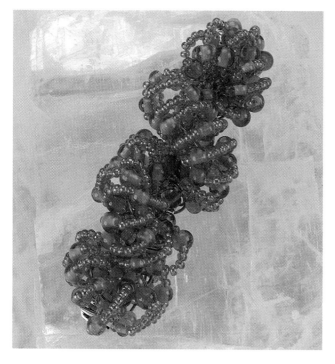

You Will Need for Both Barrettes

- Seed beads, size 11, in color to match wire
- Decorative glass beads, in color to match wire
- Twist n' Curl and small and large metal rods
- Round Nose Pliers
- Flat Nose Pliers
- Nylon Jaw Pliers
- Wire Cutter
- Barrette

You Will Need for Brown Barrette

- 24 gauge wire, Bare Copper
- 22 gauge wire, Brown

You Will Need for Purple Barrette

- 24 gauge wire, Tinned Copper
- 26 gauge wire, Tinned Copper

Brown Barrette

1. Thread seed beads and decorative beads onto a bare piece of wire in any pattern desired, leaving approximately 2" at both ends without beads.

2. Using the Twist n' Curl and large metal rod twist the entire length of beaded wire; you will end up with a coiled piece that fills the entire rod.

3. Use an additional piece of bare wire (as the core) and the Twist n' Curl to form a double coil bead.

4. Remove the coil from the rod. Attach the coil to the barrette with brown wire.

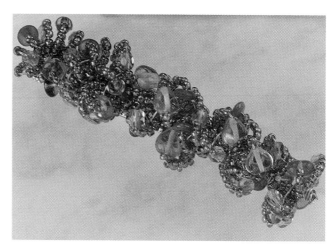

Purple Barrette

Follow the instructions for the Brown Barrette, except:
- Use 24 gauge tinned copper wire.
- Use the small metal rod for Steps 1 and 3.
- Attach the coil to the barrette with 26 gauge wire.

Beaded Brooches

Designed by Lauren Johnston

Dainty beaded brooches are the perfect accent for a jacket lapel.

You Will Need for Both Brooches
- Seed beads, size 11, in color to match wire
- Twist n' Curl and small metal rod
- Round Nose Pliers
- Flat Nose Pliers
- Nylon Jaw Pliers
- Wire Cutter
- Pin back

You Will Need for Brown Brooch
- 18 gauge wire, Natural
- 24 gauge wire, Bare Copper

You Will Need for Purple Brooch
- 24 gauge wire, Tinned Copper or Black
- 20 gauge wire, Black
- 2 decorative glass beads, purple

Brown Brooch

1 Thread brown seed beads onto a piece of bare copper wire.

2 Using the Twist n' Curl twist the beaded wire to make a single coil bead until you have a bead that is approximately 1-1/4" long.

3 Cut approximately 16" of natural wire and make a spiral in one end, using 1/2" of the wire.

4 Thread the 1-1/4" coiled piece onto the straight end of the spiraled wire. Make a spiral with the remaining end of wire.

Purple Brooch

1 Thread purple beads onto a 24" piece of tinned copper or black wire. **Note:** Because you will need to thread on approximately 24" of beads, you may want to leave the wire on the spool.

2 Using the Twist n' Curl coil the beaded wire.

3 Cut a piece of 20 gauge black wire to thread through the center of the beaded coil, allowing enough at either end to create an anchor loop.

4 Form your beaded coil into "S" shape, or other desired curve, and make an anchor loop at each end.

5 Attach a decorative glass bead to each anchor loop.

Copper Coiled Bracelet

The single coils in this unique bracelet enclosed frosted beads. You can hand-twist two pieces of wire to make one-of-a-kind single coils.

You Will Need

- 22 gauge wire, Copper
- 12 frosted glass beads, white
- 4 glass beads, white, various shapes
- Twist n' Curl and large metal rod
- 2 premade jump rings and clasp, silver
- Round Nose Pliers
- Wire Cutter

1 Make four simple bead links with the four glass beads.

2 Make eight wire jump rings; these will be used to join the components in the later steps.

3 Using the frosted glass beads, make three bead links (each link will use four beads).

4 Using the Twist n' Curl make three single coils, each about 1" long.

5 Slide one bead link made in Step 3 through a single coil; the single coil with enclose the bead link. Repeat this for the remaining two bead links and single coils.

6 To assemble the bracelet start with one premade jump ring; to this, attach a jump ring made in Step 2. Now connect both the end of a bead link and coil to the jump ring. Connect a jump ring to the other end of the bead link and coil.

7 Now add two bead links made in Step 1, connected with jump rings. Add a bead link and coil combination, then alternate with the remaining bead links until all components have been used.

8 To complete the bracelet, attach the final premade jump ring and clasp to the final bead link.

Twisted Coil Bracelet

This bracelet is made up of two single coils, each one in a different color of wire. For more excitement, you can select a third color of wire for the clasp.

You Will Need

- 20 gauge wire, Red, Gold, Black
- Twist n' Curl and small metal rod
- Round Nose Pliers
- Wire Cutter

1 Make two single coils, each 10" long.

2 Measure and cut two 12" pieces of wire; these pieces will be used to make the clasp and hook. Insert one piece of wire through one of the long coils.

3 Attach one end of the wire running through the coil to the handle of the Twist n' Curl. Wrap the wire around the bar and make a 1/4" long coil. Remove it from the tool and cut off the excess wire at the beginning of the small coil. The rest of the wire should still be running through the long coil.

4 Make another small coil with the wire sticking out of the other end of the long coil. Cut off the excess wire after the small coil.

5 Use the other 12" piece of straight wire to make the hook.

6 Insert the other end of the clasp wire through the small 1/4" coil at one end of the long coil. Do not run the wire through the long coil attached to the small coil; instead, bring the wire through the other 10" long coil that you set aside in Step 3.

7 With your fingers, twist the two long coils together. When the coils are completely twisted together, bring the straight wire sticking out of one of the long coils through the short coil at the end of the bracelet.

8 Use the remaining wire to create the clasp.

Making Long Coils

To make a coil that is longer than the length of the bar, make a coil as long as you can, then slip it off of the bar. Carefully bend open the coil between two loops near the unfinished end and insert the bar through the end of the coil again. Now you can continue wrapping the wire around the bar until you have a coil of the desired length. When you remove the coil from the bar, squeeze the opened loops together again.

Project 20 Wrapped Coil Set

Wrapped double coil beads are used in this classy set of jewelry.

You Will Need
- 20 and 22 gauge wire, Copper and Black
- Twist n' Curl and small and large metal rods
- Round Nose Pliers
- Wire Cutter

Bracelet

1 Using the small rod and 22 gauge wire, begin each double coil with a single coil that is 4" long. To alternate colors of beads on this bracelet, make four coils of one color and three coils of the other. Complete each double coil bead with the other color of wire, making a contrasting 1/4" coil at each end of the bead. Make a total of seven beads.

2 To wrap each double coil bead, slide the bead back onto the bar. Attach the same color wire as used on the end of the coils into the hole in the handle. Begin to wrap the new wire around the bead, covering the end coil completely. Bring the wire around the center of the double coil as well, letting the wire fall between each row of the double coil. Continue to wrap the wire around the other end coil. Remove the wrapped double coil bead and cut off the excess wire.

3 Turn out the last loops of each end coil with pliers.

4 Cut a 4-1/2" piece of wire and make a hook at one end. After the hook, make a loop. Keeping the loop on the nose of the pliers, wrap the wire around the nose again to make a double loop.

5 Cut a 2-1/2" piece of wire and make the clasp at one end. Make a double loop after the clasp.

6 With both colors of excess wire, make wire jump rings; make eight wire rings of each color.

7 To assemble the bracelet, attach one wire ring of each color onto the double loop of the clasp. Also attach both rings onto the end loop of one of the wrapped double coils. Continue to attach each wrapped double coil onto the bracelet with two wire rings. Alternate colors of the coils as you go. **Important:** With pliers, squeeze the end loops of each wrapped double coil closed after hooking it onto the wire rings. Complete the bracelet by adding the hook.

Necklace

Follow the instructions for the bracelet, but use the 20 gauge wire, the large rod, and make 14 wrapped double coil beads.

Earrings

1 Make two ear wires.

2 Follow Steps 1 and 2 for the bracelet to make one double coil bead for each earring.

3 Attach one coil to each ear wire.

Curls and Beads Set

The loosely curled strands of this unique set are truly one-of-a-kind!

You Will Need
- 22 gauge wire, Black
- 46 pony beads, 1/8" wide, red
- Twist n' Curl and small metal rod
- Round Nose Pliers
- Wire Cutter

Necklace

1 Measure and cut two 27" pieces of wire. Make an anchor loop at the end of each piece. Bring the straight end of each piece of wire through 12 beads.

2 Attach the straight end of one of the wires to the handle of the Twist n' Curl. Begin to wrap wire around the rod, making a tight single coil. Slide a bead up to the coil on the bar when desired, then continue to wrap the wire as before. After the last bead, open the loop at the end and coil the rest of the wire.

3 Take the beaded coil off of the rod. Holding the end of the coil, stretch it until it measures 18" long. The beads will tend to slide around the opened coil, so you may want to twist or pinch some of the loops to "trap" the beads along the wire.

4 Using the other 27" piece of wire, repeat Steps 2 and 3 and make another curled strand.

5 Cut a 4-1/2" piece of wire and make a hook at one end. After the hook, use the round nose pliers to make a loop. Keeping the loop on the nose of the pliers, wrap the wire around the nose again to make a double loop.

6 Cut a 2-1/2" piece of wire and make the clasp at one end. Make a double loop after the clasp.

7 To assemble the necklace, bring one end of each of the curled strands through the double loop of the clasp. Loop the ends around the double loop, then twist underneath to secure.

8 Bring the other two ends of the curled strands through the double loop of the catch. Twist to secure.

Bracelet

Follow the instructions for the necklace, except use pieces of wire that are approximately 14" long and 16 beads.

Earrings

1 Make two ear wires.

2 For each earring, curl a short piece of wire with three beads on it and attach to the ear wire.

Coils and Cord Necklace

What could be easier—or more attractive—than stringing single coil beads and glass beads onto a cord? This is a perfect project for children!

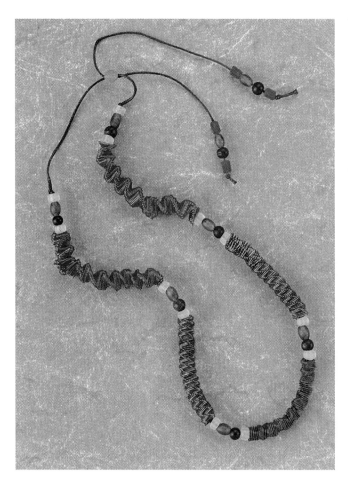

You Will Need

◎ 22 gauge wire, Red, Magenta, Copper, Dark Green
◎ 33" jewelry cord, black
◎ 33 frosted glass beads, various shapes and colors
◎ Twist n' Curl and various rods
◎ Wire Cutter
◎ Needle

1 Using the Twist n' Curl and the square and triangular rods, make five single coils; make two red, two copper, and one magenta. Make each bead approximately 3" long.

2 Using the small metal rod, make five single coils with the green wire.

3 Thread four glass beads onto the cord. Now thread on a single green coil; over that, place one of the larger coils. Continue threading on glass beads and single coils onto the cord; reserve nine beads for the following steps.

4 Using the needle, thread both cords through one bead, with one cord end coming in from the left side, and the other end from the right.

5 Now string four beads onto each cord end. Knot the ends of the cord.

6 To adjust the length of the necklace, simply pull on the two knotted ends of the cord; they will slide through the central bead placed in Step 4.

Green Cuff

Designed by Elaine Schmidt

This bracelet would be great for evening wear. For an extra-special look, and added stability, hand-twist two pieces of wire together.

You Will Need

- 20 and 24 gauge wire, Dark Green
- 17 round glass beads, 9 green and 8 white
- Round Nose Pliers
- Nylon Jaw Pliers
- Wire Cutter

1 Cut two pieces of 20 gauge wire, each about 9" long.

2 Make a loose spiral in each end of both pieces of wire.

3 Wrap the end of the 24 gauge wire around one piece of 9" wire a couple of times to secure. Once it is secure, slide a green glass bead onto the wire. Now wrap the wire around the other 9" piece of wire to secure; the green bead will now be enclosed between the two pieces of wire.

4 Continue sliding glass beads onto the wire, alternating green and white beads, and securing the wire to both 9" pieces of wire. After you have used all of the beads, secure the end of the 24 gauge wire tightly to one of the 9" pieces.

5 Bend the bracelet into a "U" shape.

Fiesta Jewelry Set

This set is shown in wire of various colors. Have fun coming up with your own unique color combinations.

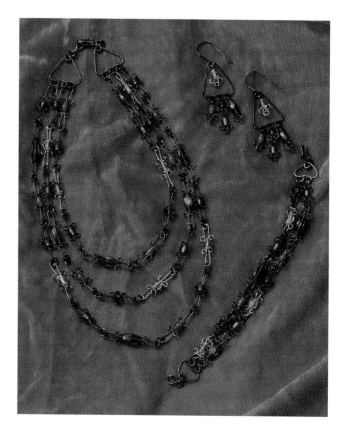

You Will Need

◎ 22 gauge wire, various colors
◎ 48 beads, various shapes and colors
◎ Jig and pegs
◎ Round Nose Pliers
◎ Wire Cutter

1 Place the jig over jig pattern A, lining up the holes of the jig with the circles on the pattern. Place a small peg at each position.

2 Cut an 8" piece of wire and create an anchor loop at one end.

3 Slip the anchor loop onto peg A. Bring the wire around peg B with your fingers. As you do this, loop the wire tightly around, pushing it down to the base of the peg.

4 Lift the wire with the two loops off of the jig. Bring the end of the wire through a bead, sliding the bead up to the last loop made.

5 Reposition the wire shape onto the jig by turning the shape over so that the top loop fits over peg A

and the loop above the bead fits on peg F. **Note:** The position of pegs C, D, and E may have to be adjusted based on the size of your bead. If the bead is too long for the space provided on the jig, lower those three pegs to accommodate it.

6 Wrap the wire around peg E. Continue around peg D, wrapping the wire around so that it circles the peg completely. Lift the shape off of the jig again.

7 Turn the shape around again and reposition it onto the jig so that the loops fall on pegs A, B, C, and D. Wrap the wire around peg E, then slide the wire through the bead again.

8 Once again, lift the shape off of the jig. Turn the shape over and reposition it on the jig so that the loops fall on all of the pegs, except for peg B. Wrap the wire around peg B, then complete the shape by circling around peg A again. Lift the shape off of the jig and cut off the excess wire. Tighten the final loop.

9 Repeat Steps 1 to 8 an additional 35 times for a total of 36 beaded wire shapes. Vary the colors of the wire and the beads used with each shape.

10 This necklace has three rows of beaded wire shapes. The rows are joined at both ends of the necklace with a wire connector. To create this shape, use jig pattern B. Place a small peg at each position. Cut 7" of wire and create an anchor loop at one end.

11 Slip the anchor loop onto peg A. Bring the wire around the outside of peg B, then wrap it around peg C.

12 Continue to wrap the wire around pegs D and E. Bring the wire around the outside of peg F and complete the shape around peg A again. Lift the shape off of the jig, cut off the excess wire, and tighten the final loop. Repeat Steps 10 to 12 and create a second connector.

13 To create the clasp, lay the jig over jig pattern C. Place a small peg at position A and a medium peg at position B. Cut a 4" piece of wire and create an anchor loop at one end.

14 Slip the anchor loop onto peg A. Circle around peg B, then around peg A again to complete the clasp. Lift the shape off of the jig, cut off the excess wire, and tighten the final loop.

15 To create the hook, lay the jig over jig pattern D. Place a small peg at both positions. Cut a 6" piece of wire and create an anchor loop at one end.

16 Slip the anchor loop onto peg A. Circle around peg B, then around peg A again to complete the hook. Lift the shape off the jig, cut off the excess wire, and tighten the final loop.

17 Use pliers to bend the wire shape in half. Now bend the looped end up slightly.

18 With excess wire, create 41 wire jump rings.

19 To assemble the necklace, twist open one wire ring and use the opened ring to attach the small loop of the clasp to the top of the triple row connector. Twist the ring closed again. Attach a beaded wire shape to each of the bottom loops of the connector with wire rings. Continue to attach the rest of the wire shapes with wire rings, creating three long rows and alternating shapes and colors of beads and wire as you make each row. The top row should have 10 shapes, the middle row 12 shapes, and the bottom row 14 shapes. Attach the end of each row to the other triple row connector and complete the necklace with the other end of the clasp.

Bracelet
Follow the instructions for the necklace, but create only 14 wire shapes to connect with wire jump rings.

Earrings
1 Make two ear wires.

2 Create two clasps from Step 13 of the necklace and a total of eight wire shapes to dangle from the clasps.

3 Assemble the earrings by hanging the four wire shapes from each "clasp." Attach to the ear wires.

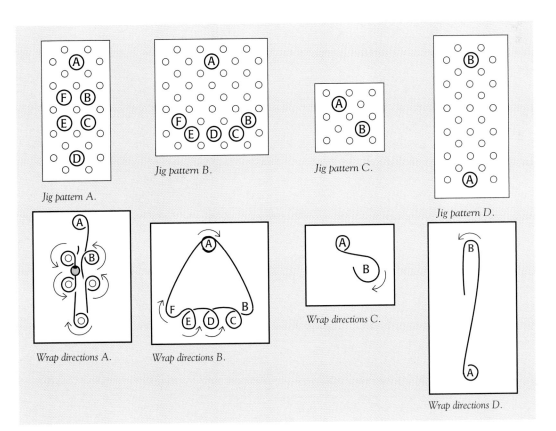

Jig pattern A.

Jig pattern B.

Jig pattern C.

Jig pattern D.

Wrap directions A.

Wrap directions B.

Wrap directions C.

Wrap directions D.

Figure-eight Draped Set

Nothing is more elegant than a draped necklace. With its cascade of wire and beads, this necklace is no exception.

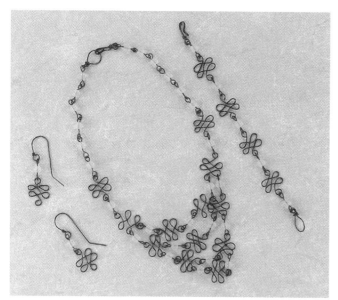

Necklace

1 Place the jig over jig pattern A, lining up the holes of the jig with the circles on the pattern. Place a small peg at each position.

2 Cut a 5" piece of wire and create an anchor loop at one end.

3 Slip the anchor loop onto peg A. Bring the wire around peg B with your fingers. As you do this, loop the wire tightly around, pushing it down to the base of the peg.

4 Wrap the wire around pegs C, D, and E. Complete the shape by wrapping the wire around peg F. Lift the shape off of the jig and cut off the excess wire. Tighten the final loop. Repeat Steps 1 to 4 an additional 11 times for a total of 12 wire shapes.

5 Cut 29 pieces of wire, each 1-1/2" long, and make 29 bead links, each with one round bead.

6 To create the clasp, lay the jig over jig pattern B. Place a small peg at positions A and C. Place a large peg at position B.

7 Cut a 5" piece of wire and create an anchor loop at one end. Slip the anchor loop onto peg A.

You Will Need
- 10 ft. of 22 gauge wire, Red
- 36 round beads, 4mm wide, white
- Jig and pegs
- Round Nose Pliers
- Bent Chain Nose Pliers
- Wire Cutter

Wrap the wire around peg B. Complete the shape by wrapping the wire around peg C.

8 Lift the shape off of the jig but do not cut off the excess wire. Using bent chain nose pliers, twist one small loop at the bottom of the clasp a full 90 degrees toward the other small loop. Now twist the other loop to meet the first one.

9 Using the excess wire at the top of one of the loops, wrap the wire tightly around the base of the large loop of the clasp a few times. Cut off the excess wire after wrapping. Use bent chain nose pliers to push the end inward.

10 To create the hook, lay the jig over jig pattern C. Place a small peg at all three positions. Cut a 6" piece of wire and create an anchor loop at one end.

11 Slip the anchor loop onto peg A. Bring the wire around peg B, then complete the shape by circling around peg C. Lift the shape off the jig but do not cut off the excess wire.

12 As described in Steps 8 and 9, twist each of the small loops toward each other and wrap the excess wire around the base of the long loop. Use your pliers to bend the long loop of the hook in half. Now bend the looped end up slightly.

13 To assemble the necklace, twist open one loop of a bead link and attach it to the small loops of the clasp. Twist the loop closed again. Attach another bead link to the first bead link. Continue adding bead links until you have made a chain of six bead links. Attach a wire shape to the last bead link. Add

a bead link after the wire shape. Continue alternating bead links and wire shapes until there are six wire shapes on the necklace. Add six more bead links, completing the row with the other part of the clasp.

14 Attach a second row of wire shapes to the necklace with bead links; two should be centered on the necklace and have a total of three wire shapes. Row three centers under row two and has a total of two wire shapes. Row four centers under row three and has one wire shape.

Bracelet

Follow the instructions for the necklace, but create only four wire shapes to connect with wire jump rings.

Earrings

1 Create two ear wires.

2 For each earring, make a wire shape as described in Steps 1 to 4 of the necklace.

3 Now make a bead link as described in Step 5.

4 To assemble each earring, twist open the loops at the ends of the bead link. Hook the bead link onto the small loop of the ear wire and twist the opened loop closed. Hook the other end of the bead link onto the wire shape and twist the loop closed.

Ring

1 Use jig pattern A to create the pattern, starting with an anchor loop.

2 After completing the design, lift the wire from the jig and place loop F onto peg A; make as many repetitions of the pattern as needed to fit around your finger.

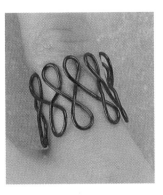

3 Use pliers to connect the beginning and ending anchor loops to create a circle.

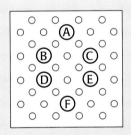

Jig pattern A.

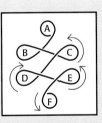

Wrap directions A.

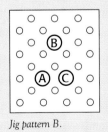

Jig pattern B.

Wrap directions B.

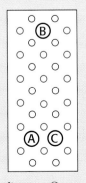

Jig pattern C.

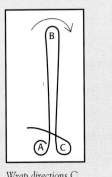

Wrap directions C.

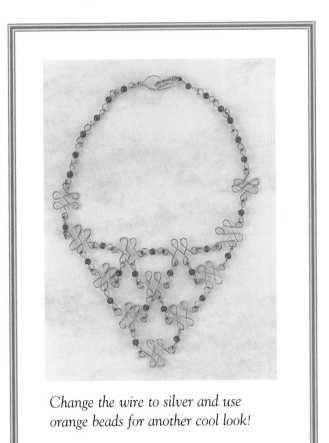

Change the wire to silver and use orange beads for another cool look!

Project

26 Barrettes

To wear one of these unique barrettes, pull your hair into a ponytail with one hand while shaping the barrette around it. Then, insert the straight "stick" through the two end loops, behind your hair.

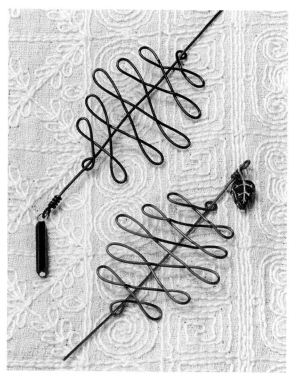

You Will Need

◎ 18 gauge wire, Black or Red
◎ 1 small bead (any shape), black or red
◎ Jig and pegs
◎ Round Nose Pliers
◎ File
◎ Wire Cutter

3 Slip the anchor loop onto peg A. Bring the wire around peg B with your fingers. As you do this, loop the wire tightly around, pushing it down to the base of the peg.

4 Wrap the wire around the rest of the pegs. Lift the shape off of the jig and cut off the excess wire. Tighten the final loop.

5 To create the barrette stick, cut 6" of wire. Measure 1" from the end and make a wrapped loop with your pliers at this point. Below the loop, wrap the short end of the wire around the long end of the wire a few times. Cut off any excess wire. File the edges of the barrette stick to make them smooth.

6 Cut a 2" piece of wire, make a loop at the end, slide on the bead, and make another loop after the bead to create a bead link.

7 To assemble the barrette, hook one opened loop of the bead link to the loop at the end of the barrette stick. Squeeze the loop closed.

1 Place the jig over the jig pattern, lining up the holes of the jig with the circles on the pattern. Place a small peg at positions A and L. Place a medium peg at all other positions.

2 Cut a 24" piece of wire and create an anchor loop at one end.

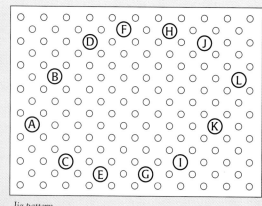

Jig pattern.

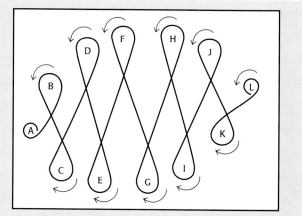

Wrap directions.

Snake Coil Set

To make this bracelet, one long piece of wire is inserted through different colors of single coils and an assortment of small round beads.

You Will Need

- 26 gauge wire, various colors
- Approx. 50 round beads, various colors and sizes
- Twist n' Curl and small metal rod
- Round Nose Pliers
- Wire Cutter
- File
- 2-3/4" diameter unopened metal can
- Pre-made hoop earrings, gold

Bracelet

1. Use a variety of wire colors to make seven 3" long single coils.

2. Measure and cut a 27" piece of wire. Make an anchor loop at one end. After the loop, string one round bead onto the wire.

3. Bring the straight end of the wire halfway through a coil, letting the end stick out of the middle of the coil. Bring the wire through a bead, then continue through the rest of the coil. Push the bead up into the coil to lock it in place and pull the wire that is running through the coil to straighten it out. Slide the coil along the wire onto the looped end of the bracelet.

4. After the coil, slide on a bead. Then repeat Step 3 with another coil. With some of the coils, you may want to insert two or three beads at shorter intervals along the coil.

5. The last coil may be too long for the piece of wire. Cut it down to size, leaving room after the coil for one final bead and a loop. With pliers, bend the end of the wire into a loop as you did at the beginning of the bracelet.

6. To shape the bracelet, use the metal can. Hold one end of the bracelet against the side of the can and wrap the rest of the bracelet around it, shaping the wire as you go.

7. Make two bead links, each with a 1-1/2" piece of wire and three beads. Attach the bead links to the end loops of the bracelet.

Earrings

For these earrings, you will simply string two single coils, in colors that match the bracelet, and glass beads onto the pre-made hoop earrings.

Here's the bracelet in another color scheme.

Red and Silver Coil Necklace

Small triple coil beads are the focal point of this fun necklace.

You Will Need

- 20 gauge wire, Bare (silver) and Red
- 6 round beads, blue
- 2 premade jump rings and 1 clasp, silver
- Twist n' Curl and small metal rod
- Round Nose Pliers
- Wire Cutter

1 Make five triple coil beads; use red wire for the first and second coils and bare wire for the final triple coil. Each bead should be about 1-1/2" long, with 1" left at each end. Make a double loop at each end of each triple coil.

2 Using red wire, make 12 small single coils, each 1/2" long.

3 To make the six bead links, cut a piece of wire that is 3-1/2" long. At one end, make a double loop. Slide on one single coil, a blue bead, and another single coil. Make a double loop with the remaining wire.

4 Make 10 jump rings with red wire. Use these to connect the necklace components in Step 5.

5 To assemble the necklace, join three bead links together. Then link the five triple coil beads together, connecting the first one to the last bead link placed. Now connect the three remaining bead links to the final triple coil bead.

6 Attach the premade jump rings and clasp to the end bead links.

Project 29 Ponytail Holder

This unique hair accessory can be made in five simple steps!

You Will Need

- 18 gauge Red, Gray, or Brown
- 1 ponytail holder, red, gray, or brown
- Jig and pegs
- Round Nose Pliers
- Wire Cutter

1. Place the jig over the jig pattern, lining up the holes of the jig with the circles on the pattern. Place a small peg at positions A, B, C, D, I, J, K, and L. Place a medium peg at positions E, F, G, and H.

2. Create an anchor loop at one end of the wire.

3. Slip the anchor loop onto peg A. Bring the wire around peg B with your fingers. As you do this, loop the wire tightly around, pushing it down to the base of the peg.

4. Wrap the wire around the rest of the pegs. Lift the shape off of the jig and cut off the excess wire. Tighten the final loop.

5. To attach the wire shape onto a ponytail holder, open the two outside loops of the wire shape and hook each loop on the band of the ponytail holder. Squeeze the loops closed again.

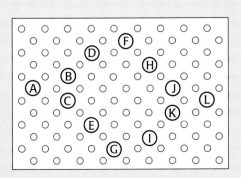

Jig pattern.

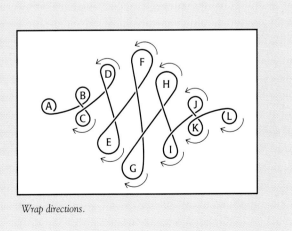

Wrap directions.

Sampler Necklace 1

This necklace is made up of a variety of coils. Many different colors of wire can be used with an assortment of different size beads. Use the small metal rod for most of the coils in this necklace, but feel free to experiment. The center design is made with a larger round rod.

You Will Need
- 20 and 24 gauge wire, various colors
- Numerous beads, various sizes and colors
- Twist n' Curl with a variety of rods
- Round Nose Pliers
- Nylon Jaw Pliers
- Wire Cutter

1 Use two different colors of wire to make a triple coil bead. Make a second triple coil bead, using different colors of wire.

2 Make a 3-1/2" single coil, remove it from the Twist n' Curl, and cut off the excess wire. Begin a second coil on the tool with another color of wire. After you make a 1" coil, slide the first coil back onto the bar, pushing it up against the new coil. Use the wire on the bar to wrap around the first coil. When you reach the end of the first coil, use the wire to create another 1" coil. At this point you should have what looks like a long two-colored coil with the center section wrapped with wire. Create a double coil using this two-colored coil as the center.

3 Repeat Step 2 and make another double coil bead the same way, but use a different combination of colors.

4 For another type of coil, cut a 24" piece of wire and make a loop at one end. Slide 25 small beads onto the wire and make a single coil. Make a double coil with the beaded single coil as its center. Now make this double coil into a triple coil bead.

5 Repeat Step 4 and make a second triple coil bead with a beaded center. Again, vary the colors of wire used.

6 Make two 7" long single coils, using a different color of wire for each. Now, choose two new col-

ors of wire and slip the end of one color through a 7" coil and the end of the other color through the other 7" coil. Attach the ends of both pieces of wire to the handle of the tool. (Try to insert both ends into the hole of the handle. If they do not fit together, insert one end, then twist the other piece of wire around the attached wire to keep them both secure.) Wrap both pieces of wire around the bar at once, making a striped coil, 1-1/2" long.

7 After the striped coil, slide the two 7" long coils up to the bar and, with your fingers, twist the coils together. Wrap this twisted coil around the bar. Make this into a triple coil bead with the twisted bead as its center.

8 Repeat Steps 6 and 7 to make another triple coil bead with a twisted center.

9 To make another type of bead, start with a double coil made out of a 7" single coil center with a 1-1/2" beaded coil at each end. Using this double coil as its center, make a triple coil bead. Repeat this step to make a second triple coil bead.

10 To make the center coils of the necklace, use the large metal rod. Attach one piece of wire to the handle of the tool. Leave about 2" of straight wire before coiling the wire around the bar. Make a 1" long coil. Remove the coil from the bar and leave about 2" of wire before cutting off the excess wire. Grab the end loops of the coil and stretch the coil out until it measures 3". Slide about six beads onto the coil, letting them settle along the opened coil.

11 Make a spiral at each end of the coil. Bend the coil into the shape of an arc.

12 Repeat Step 10 and make another opened coil with beads, only this time, stretch a 3/4" coil out to 2-1/2", then add your beads. Cut off the excess wire at each end of the opened coil, leaving about 1/2" at each end. Bring one end of this coil through the center of one of the spirals made in Step 11.

With pliers, bend the wire around to create a loop. Attach the other end of the two coils the same way.

13 The hook is a 2" piece of shaped wire. Use pliers to make a small loop at each end of the wire, then bend the center of the wire around.

14 The clasp is a 4" piece of wire made into a spiral at one end and a small loop at the other end.

15 This necklace is assembled in two halves. Separate each pair of the coil beads made in Steps 1 through 9 into two sets. Assemble one half of the necklace first with one set of these coils.

16 Cut a 14" piece of wire. Bring the end of the wire through six small round beads and loop the beads around, twisting the wire under the loop to secure. Attach the catch of the clasp to the loop of beads.

17 Make a 1-1/2" single coil on the small metal rod. Remove the coil from the rod and cut off the excess wire. Bring the wire attached to the clasp through the single coil, adding about four beads to the coil as you bring the wire through. Slide the beaded coil along the wire until it meets the loop of beads after the clasp.

18 Now string one set of coiled beads onto the wire.

19 After the last coil, bring the end of the wire through three small beads. Bring the wire through the spiral at one end of the center decoration. Add three more small beads to the wire then loop the beads around and twist the end of the wire under the loop to secure. Cut off the excess wire.

20 Repeat Step 16, attaching a new piece of 14" wire to the hook with a loop of beads. Repeat Steps 17 to 19 and continue to create the other half of the necklace, attaching the end of this new half to the other spiral on the center coils.

31 $\mathcal{S}$ampler Necklace 2

This sampler necklace also is made up of many coils and types of beads, but you will also be making jigged designs to link the coils and beads together.

You Will Need

◎ Wire, in various gauges and colors
◎ 15 glass beads, various shapes, sizes, and colors
◎ Jig and pegs
◎ Twist n' Curl and various rods
◎ Round Nose Pliers
◎ Nylon Jaw Pliers
◎ Wire Cutter

each end. If desired, add beads to the ends of the wire prior to making the anchor loops in the wire ends.

2 Make five double coils beads using various colors or wire and the small metal rod. Each completed bead should be about 1-1/2" to 2" long. Slip each double coil bead onto another piece of wire, which will function as a bead link; make an anchor loop in each end. If desired, add beads to the ends of the wire prior to making the anchor loops in the wire ends.

3 Make two single coil beads with two different larger rods; these beads should each be about 1-1/2" long. Slip each single coil onto another piece of wire, which will function as a bead link; make an anchor loop in each end. If desired, add beads to the ends of the wire prior to making the anchor loops in the wire ends.

4 Place the jig over jig pattern A, lining up the holes of the jig with the circles on the pattern. Place a small peg at each position.

5 Make an anchor loop in one end of one color of wire. Slip this loop onto peg A and follow the

1 Using various colors of wire and the small metal rod, make three triple coil beads. Each completed bead should be about 1-1/2" to 2" long. Slip each completed bead onto another piece of wire, which will function as a bead link; make an anchor loop in

wrap directions. Tighten the final loop, cut the excess wire, and slip the design off of the jig. Repeat this procedure with another color of wire.

6 Use jig pattern A to make two additional designs, but this time leave about 1" of wire at each end of the design. When the design is completed, make a spiral on each end.

7 Place the jig over jig pattern B, lining up the holes of the jig with the circles on the pattern. Place a small peg at each position.

8 Make an anchor loop in one end of one color of wire. Slip this loop onto peg A and follow the wrap directions. Tighten the final loop, cut the excess wire, and slip the design off of the jig.

9 Make 18 wire jump rings with various colors of wire.

10 Make one bead link with two 1/4" coils and one glass bead.

11 Make three spiral eye pins. On two of these pins, slip on two glass beads and then make a final loop. For the final pin, slip on a glass bead, one triple coil bead, another glass bead and then make a final loop. Reserve these three eye pins for Step 16.

12 The hook is a 2" piece of shaped wire. Use pliers to make a small loop at each end of the wire, then bend the center of the wire around.

13 The catch of the clasp is a 4" piece of wire made into a spiral at one end and a small loop at the other end.

14 To assemble the necklace, begin linking the components together in any arrangement desired. Join the first piece to the clasp with a jump ring; continue joining pieces together with jump rings. Make sure that the piece made in Step 8 (from jig pattern B) is directly in the middle of the necklace.

15 Attach the final bead to the hook.

16 Using the remaining jump rings, attach the three spiral eye pins made in Step 11 to the jigged design in the middle of the necklace. Attach the two shorter pins with glass beads to the outermost loops of the design and the pin with the triple coil bead onto the middle loop.

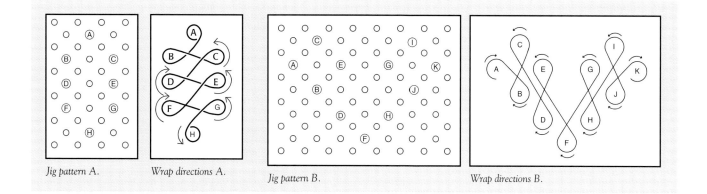

Jig pattern A.   Wrap directions A.   Jig pattern B.   Wrap directions B.

Triple Coil Set

Two colors of wire make up the five triple coil beads of this necklace. The earrings incorporate simple single coils and beads, while the bracelet is one continuous double coil.

You Will Need

- 24 gauge wire, Copper and Black
- 16 round beads, 1/8" wide, black
- 8 round beads, 5/16" wide, copper
- Twist n' Curl and small metal rod
- Round Nose Pliers
- Wire Cutter

Necklace

1 Make four triple coils beads with both colors of wire and one triple coil bead from one color only. Begin each triple coil with a single coil that is 12" long. To make a coil that is longer than the length of the bar, see page 45.

2 Cut five 3" pieces of wire. Make a loop at one end of a piece. Keeping the loop on the nose of the pliers, wrap the wire around the nose again to make a double loop. Insert the wire after the double loop through a triple coil bead. Make a double loop at the other end of the bead and cut off any excess wire. Complete each triple coil bead this way.

3 Make sixteen 1/4" single coils with either color of wire.

4 Cut eight 3" pieces of wire. Make a double loop at the end of each piece. After the double loop, slide on a 1/4" coil, a small bead, a large bead, a small

bead, and another 1/4" coil. Make a double loop at the end and cut off any excess wire. Complete eight bead links in this manner.

5 Cut a 4-1/2" piece of wire and make a hook at one end. After the hook, make a double loop.

6 Cut a 2-1/2" piece of wire and make the clasp at one end. After the clasp, make a double loop.

7 To assemble the necklace, attach the double loop of a bead link to the double loop of the clasp. To hook the double loops together, loosen one set of double loops, then slide the other set of loops along the loosened loops as you would a key on a split key ring.

8 Attach another bead link to the other side of the first link, then add a triple coil bead. Continue to alternate one bead link with one triple coil bead. Place the solid color triple coil bead in the center of the necklace. After the last triple coil bead, add two more bead links. Finish the necklace by adding the hook.

Earrings

1 Make two ear wires and two short single coils with either color of wire.

2 Slip one small bead, one large bead, a small single coil, and one final small bead onto each wire.

Bracelet

1 Make a double coil out of a 32" single coil from either color of wire.

2 Follow Steps 5 and 6 of the necklace to make a hook and a clasp.

3 Assemble the bracelet by attaching the long double coil to the hook and clasp.

33 Black Dangling Beaded Set

Dainty spirals and clear round beads add excitement to this simple linked design.

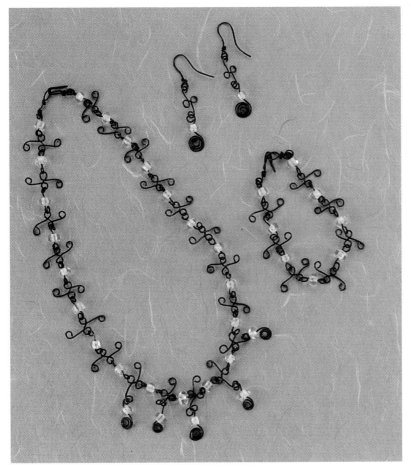

You Will Need
- 22 gauge wire, Black
- 36 round beads, 4mm wide, clear
- Jig and pegs
- Round Nose Pliers
- Nylon Jaw Pliers
- Wire Cutter

Necklace

1 Place the jig over the jig pattern, lining up the holes of the jig with the circles on the pattern. Place a small peg at each position.

2 Cut a 3" piece of wire and create an anchor loop at one end.

3 Slip the anchor loop onto peg A. Bring the wire around peg B with your fingers. As you do this, loop the wire tightly around, pushing it down to the base of the peg.

4 Wrap the wire around peg C, then peg D. Lift the shape off of the jig and cut off the excess wire. Tighten the final loop. Repeat Steps 1 to 4 an additional 16 times for a total of 17 wire shapes.

5 Cut a 1-1/2" piece of wire, make an eye loop at the end, slide on one bead, and make a final eye loop after the bead. Repeat this step until you have a total of 23 bead links.

6 Make the clasp and hook with two small pieces of wire.

7 To assemble the necklace, twist open one loop of a bead link and attach it to the small loops of the clasp. Twist the loop closed again. Open the other loop of the bead link and hook it onto a loop of a wire shape. Continue to alternate bead links with wire shapes, making a long chain of 18 bead links and

17 wire shapes. Hook the last bead link onto the hook.

8 Attach the five remaining bead links to the center five wire shapes of the necklace.

Bracelet

Follow the instructions for the necklace but make only seven beaded wire shapes. Attach the shapes as directed above.

Earrings

1 Create two ear wires.

2 For each earring, make a wire shape as described in Steps 1 to 4 of the necklace.

3 Now make a bead link as described in Step 5.

4 To assemble each earring, twist open the loop at one end of the wire shape. Hook the wire shape onto the small loop of the ear wire. Close the opened loop. Attach the bead link to the other end of the wire shape.

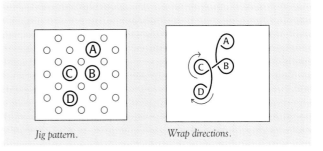

Jig pattern.   Wrap directions.

Here is the necklace and pair of earrings both made with black wire, but instead of using clear round beads, we have used square iridescent beads.

 Twisted Heart Set

Simple single coils joined by loopy spirals make up this cute necklace.
The matching earrings can be made in no time at all.

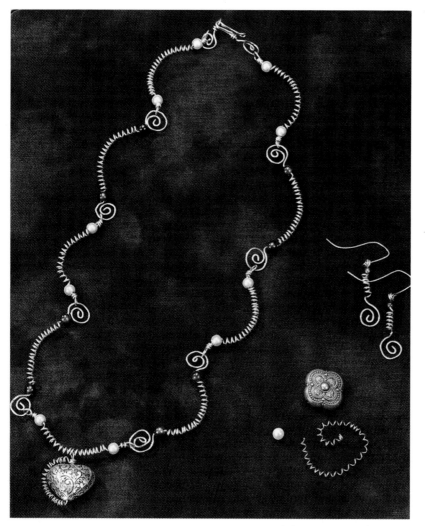

You Will Need

- 18 gauge wire, Bare (silver)
- 1 large heart bead, silver
- 10 small round beads, 3/16" wide, white
- 8 small round beads, 3/16" wide, black
- Twist n' Curl and small metal rod
- Round Nose Pliers
- Nylon Jaw Pliers
- Wire Cutter

Necklace

1. Make nine single coils, each 1-1/4" long. Leave about 1" excess wire at each end of the coils.

2. With your fingers, spread each coil to lengthen to 1-1/2" and bend the coil into an arc.

3. With five of the coils, slide a white bead onto each end of the coil. After each bead, use the pliers to make a loop, twisting the wire under the loop to secure. Cut off the excess wire.

4. With the remaining four coils, slide a black bead onto each end of the coil. After each bead, use the pliers to make a spiral with the end of the wire.

5. Make another 1-1/4" single coil, leaving 3/4" excess wire at one end and 1-1/2" excess wire at the other end.

6. Slip the 1-1/2" end of wire through the heart bead so that the coil sits at the bottom of the heart. Use the pliers to make a loop with the wire at the top of the heart.

7 Bend the coil around the side of the heart. Use the excess wire after the coil to wrap around under the loop at the top of the heart.

8 Cut a 5" piece of wire and make a hook at one end. After the hook, make a spiral.

9 Cut a 3" piece of wire and make a clasp at one end. After the clasp, make a spiral.

10 To assemble the necklace, attach the loop at one end of a coil (made in Step 3) to the spiral of the clasp. Attach the loop at the other end of the coil to the spiral of another coil (made in Step 4). Continue alternating coils, attaching the loop of one to the spiral of another. Attach the spiral of the hook to the last coil.

11 Hook the loop at the top of the heart to the middle of the center coil on the necklace.

Earrings

1 Make two ear wires.

2 Make two single coils, each about 3/4" long with an additional 3/4" on one end. Form a spiral with the excess wire.

3 Attach the single coils to the ear wires.

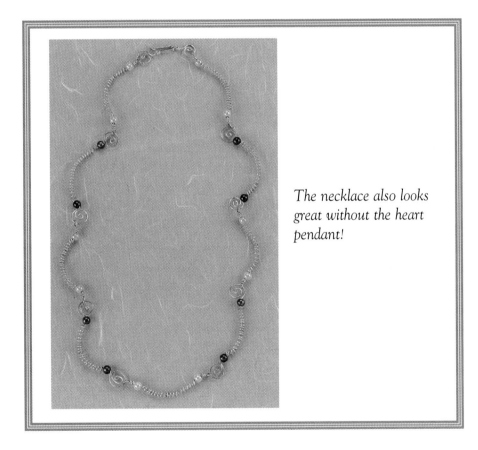

The necklace also looks great without the heart pendant!

Section 2
Projects for Your Home

Wire's most popular applications are typically jewelry, like the pieces presented in Section 1; however, what about adding coils, wire beads, and jigged designs to home décor items? Here, you will find ways to create keepsake photo frames, embellished pillows for all of your living spaces, and stunning glassware to adorn your table.

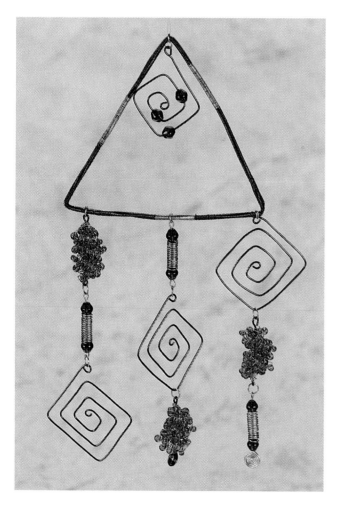

Easy Beaded Lampshade

Designed by Elaine Schmidt

Add a touch of elegance to any lampshade with wire and large glass beads.

You Will Need

- 18 gauge wire, Natural
- 12 large decorative glass beads, various colors and sizes
- 9" tall lampshade, purple
- 13-1/2" tall metal lamp base
- Needle and thread, purple
- Round Nose Pliers
- Wire Cutter

1 Make 12 freeform eye loops, with each completed shape being about 2" to 2-1/2" long. Begin each with an anchor loop, then thread a decorative bead onto each piece of wire. Use round nose pliers to bend the wire back and forth into a squiggle shape. Bend the wire at a right angle and end with another anchor loop.

2 Evenly space and stitch each eye loop onto the lower edge of the lampshade.

3 Assemble the lamp and admire!

Other Lampshade Ideas

- *Add studs or rhinestones to the lampshade with the Be-Dazzler.*
- *Wrap the lamp base with beaded wire.*
- *Take the fabric off of the lampshade and wrap the "support" with wire.*

Project 36 Pillow With Wire Charm Trim

Designed by Elaine Schmidt

Dress up any pre-made pillow with braided trim and jigged wire shapes.

You Will Need
- 20 gauge wire, Bare Copper
- 16" purchased pillow, green
- 1/2 yd. braided trim, light green
- Needle and thread, light green
- Optional: Fabric glue
- Scissors
- Jig and pegs
- Round Nose Pliers
- Wire Cutter

1 Glue or stitch the braided trim to the front of the pillow, about 5" down from the top edge. Trim any excess

2 Make 11 wire charms, following the jig patterns: make one large, four medium, and six small designs. Begin and end each charm with an anchor loop.

3 Stitch the charms onto the edge of the braided trim. Center the large charm, and evenly space the medium and small charms on each side (two medium charms on each side of the central large charm, and three small charms beside those).

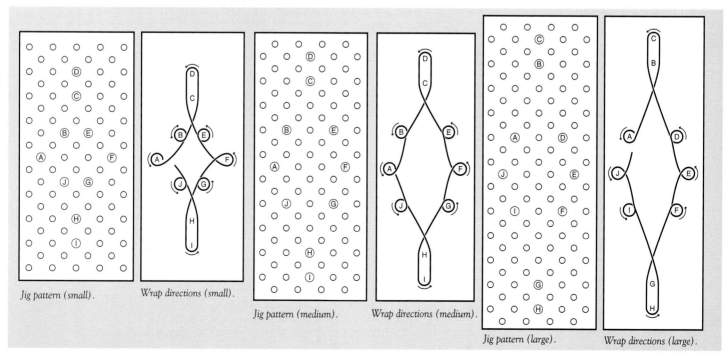

Jig pattern (small).   *Wrap directions (small).*   *Jig pattern (medium).*   *Wrap directions (medium).*   *Jig pattern (large).*   *Wrap directions (large).*

Project 37

Be-Dazzled Pillow

Designed by Lauren Johnston

Glittery rhinestones dress up this pre-made pillow.

You Will Need

- 22 gauge wire, Powder Blue
- Jig and pegs
- Be-Dazzler machine
- #20 rhinestones, blue
- #20 tiffany settings
- Round Nose Pliers
- Flat Chain Nose Pliers
- Wire Cutter
- Seam ripper
- Scissors
- Ruler
- Needle and transparent nylon thread
- Vanishing or washable fabric marker
- Fabric glue
- 12" square pillow, cream

1 Use the seam ripper to open pillow; remove the insert or stuffing so that you have a flat surface to work on.

2 Use the ruler and vanishing fabric marker to mark a diamond design on the back of the pillow front.

3 Mark every 2-1/4" with the marker along the diamond design. Also make one mark directly in the center of the pillow and four marks 2-1/4" from it (making a "cross").

4 Use the Be-Dazzler to attach a rhinestone and tiffany setting at each mark.

5 Place the jig over the jig pattern, lining up the holes of the jig with the circles on the pattern. Place a small peg at each position.

6 Follow the jig pattern, making a design with six curves. **Note:** Do not make an anchor loop at the end of the wire. Remove from the jig and stretch the design to the desired length. Make a total of 24 jigged designs.

7 Re-stuff the pillow and stitch back together with the transparent nylon thread.

8 Attach the jigged designs between the rhinestones on the pillow with fabric glue, between the rhinestones. You may need to bend the shapes slightly before applying them to the pillow to fit the shape of the pillow form or stuffing. Allow to dry completely.

Jig pattern.

Wrap directions.

Tablecloth With Beaded Fringe

Designed by Elaine Schmidt

Simple double coil beads embellish the edge of this stunning tablecloth.

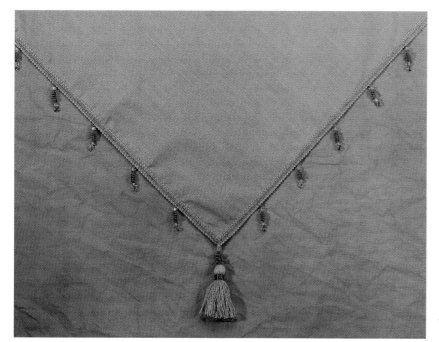

You Will Need

◎ 22 gauge wire, Brown
◎ 26 gauge wire, Lavender
◎ 54" square tablecloth, purple
◎ 6 yds. braided trim, green
◎ 4 tassels, green
◎ 96 glass pony beads, 1/4" wide, various colors
◎ Needle and thread, green
◎ Optional: Fabric glue
◎ Twist n' Curl and large and small metal rods
◎ Round Nose Pliers
◎ Nylon Jaw Pliers
◎ Wire Cutter

1 Stitch or glue the braided trim around the edge of the tablecloth.

2 Make four double coil beads, each 1" long, for the tassels with the Twist n' Curl. Use the large round metal rod and lavender wire for the first coil. Use the small metal rod and brown wire for the second double coil.

3 Thread the wire beads onto the top of the tassels. To do this, cut a short length of scrap wire and fold it in half through the tassel loop. Use this as a needle to thread the bead onto the loop.

4 Wrap the neck of each tassel with brown wire.

5 Stitch an embellished tassel to each corner of the tablecloth.

6 Make 48 double coil beads, each 1" long, with lavender and brown wire. Use the small metal rod for both coils.

7 Make a spiral eye pin for each bead, as shown on page 14. Thread a glass bead, a wire bead, and another glass bead onto each eye pin. Form an anchor loop at the top of the pin.

8 Evenly space the beads around the edge of the tablecloth. Use a few hand stitches to secure the top loop of each bead to the braided trim.

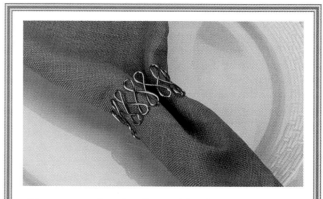

You can make simple napkin rings to accompany the tablecloth by following the instructions on page 74.

Be-Dazzled Table Runner

Designed by Lauren Johnston

This delightful table runner can be used to dress up a spring holiday table.

You Will Need

- 22 gauge wire, Powder Blue
- Jig and pegs
- Be-Dazzler machine
- #20 rhinestones, blue
- #20 tiffany settings
- Round Nose Pliers
- Flat Chain Nose Pliers
- Wire Cutter
- Seam ripper
- Scissors
- Ruler
- Needle and transparent nylon thread
- Vanishing or washable fabric marker
- Fabric glue
- Table runner, cream

1 On the back of the table runner, use the disappearing ink pen to mark every 2-1/4" along the edge.

2 Use the Be-Dazzler to attach a rhinestone and tiffany setting at each mark.

3 Place the jig over the jig pattern on page 71, lining up the holes of the jig with the circles on the pattern. Place a small peg at each position.

4 Follow the jig pattern, making a design with six curves. **Note:** Do not make an anchor loop at the end of the wire. Remove from the jig and stretch the design to the desired length. Make enough jigged designs to go around the entire edge of the table runner.

5 Attach the jigged designs between the rhinestones by carefully stitching or gluing them in place.

40 Napkin Ring

This simple napkin ring can easily be made with a jig. For more excitement, you can beads between the loops.

You Will Need

- 18 gauge wire, Copper
- Jig and pegs
- Square napkin, cream
- Wire Cutter
- Round Nose Pliers

6 Lift the shape off of the jig and reposition the last two loops onto pegs H and I. Wrap the wire around peg J to complete the shape.

7 Lift the shape off of the jig, cut off the excess wire, and tighten the final loop. With the excess wire, create a wire jump ring.

8 To complete the napkin ring, use the round nose pliers to twist the jump ring open. Hook the opened ring onto both end loops of the wire shape, forming a circle. Twist the ring closed again.

1 Place the jig over the jig pattern, lining up the holes of the jig with the circles on the pattern. Place a small peg at each position.

2 Create an anchor loop at one end of the wire.

3 Slip the anchor loop onto peg A. Bring the wire around peg B with your fingers. As you do this, loop the wire tightly around, pushing it down to the base of the peg.

4 Wrap the wire around the pegs, continuing the pattern. Do not wrap the wire around peg J.

5 Lift the shape off of the jig and reposition the loops of wire made on pegs H and I onto pegs B and C. Continue wrapping the length of wire around pegs D to I again. Continue to lift the shape off of the jig and reposition it onto pegs B and C until you have created 11 loops on each side of the shape.

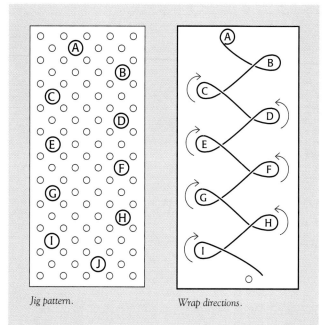

Jig pattern.   *Wrap directions.*

Beaded Napkin Ring

Continuous loops of wire and colorful pony beads will add a fun touch to your dinner table!

You Will Need

- 20 gauge wire, Copper
- 18 pony beads (6 of each), 1/4" wide, red, green, blue
- Square napkin, blue
- Jig and pegs
- Round Nose Pliers
- Wire Cutter

1 Cut one piece of wire, about 30" long.

2 Place the jig over the jig pattern, lining up the holes of the jig with the circles on the pattern. Place a small peg at each position.

3 Find the midpoint of the wire. Put the middle of the wire below the top two pegs (A and B) and loop the wire around these pegs. After making these loops, slide on one pony bead through both pieces of wire.

4 Continue following the pegs down the length of the jig, making loops and adding beads as you go. You should be able to make 13 sets of loops on the jig; when you get to the bottom, pick the entire jigged design up and place the final two loops onto pegs A and B and continue making loops. Make a total of 19 loop sets.

5 After making the final loop sets, open these loops and shape the jigged design into a circle. Join the final open loops to the two beginning loops.

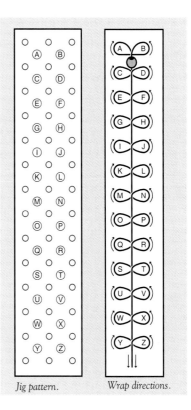

Jig pattern.   *Wrap directions.*

 Salt and Pepper Shakers

Here, you will make wire designs that fit over square and round glass bottles that can serve as salt and pepper shakers.

You Will Need

- 18 gauge wire, Red or Dark Blue
- Small bottle, square or round
- Round Nose Pliers
- Bent Chain Nose Pliers
- Wire Cutter

Square

1. Use bent chain nose pliers to turn the wire at right angles, making a square spiral. Make the design large enough to fit one side of the bottle.

2. Hold the square spiral against the side of the bottle and wrap the straight end of the wire around the bottle's neck. Circle the wire completely around the neck, then stop when it reaches the opposite side of the bottle.

3. Make another square spiral at the other end of the wire. Cut off the excess wire.

4. Repeat Steps 1 to 3 to make square spirals for the remaining two sides of the bottle.

Round

1. Make a loose spiral at one end of the wire.

2. Hold the spiral against one side of the bottle and wrap the straight end of the wire around the bottle's neck. Circle the wire completely around the neck, then stop when it reaches the opposite side of the bottle.

3. Make another loose spiral at the other end of the wire. Cut off the excess wire.

4. Repeat Steps 1 to 3 to make round spirals for the remaining two sides of the bottle.

Placecard Holder

Accents like placecards can set the mood of any special gathering. Make this swooping design in minutes!

You Will Need

- 18 gauge wire, Black
- 1 barrel-shaped bead, 3/4" long, red
- 3" x 4" piece of cardstock, cream
- Permanent marker, black
- Jig and pegs
- Round Nose Pliers

1 Place the jig over the jig pattern, lining up the holes of the jig with the circles on the pattern. Place pegs into the jig as follows: small (A), medium (B, C), large (D, E), extra-large (F, G)

2 Make an anchor loop at one end of the wire. Slip the anchor loop on peg A. Bring the wire around peg B with your fingers. Continue to wrap the wire around each of the remaining pegs the same way.

3 Remove all of the pegs on the jig except for pegs F and G. Carefully lift the loop of wire off of peg F but keep the shape attached to the jig around peg G. Rotate the shape to the right until the wire to the left of peg G lays parallel to the vertical side of the jig.

4 Holding the shape in its new position on the jig, wrap the wire around peg F. Lift the shape completely off of the jig.

5 Bring the wire through the bead. Adjust the bead along the wire until it sits vertically, under the center of the shape.

6 To create the base for the placecard holder, circle the wire under the bead, then with an even larger rotation, circle the wire around again.

7 Cut off the excess wire and make an anchor loop at the end. Adjust the wire under the bead until the shape sits securely on a flat surface.

8 Fold the cardstock in half; write the guest's name on tit. Slip the folded card into the holder.

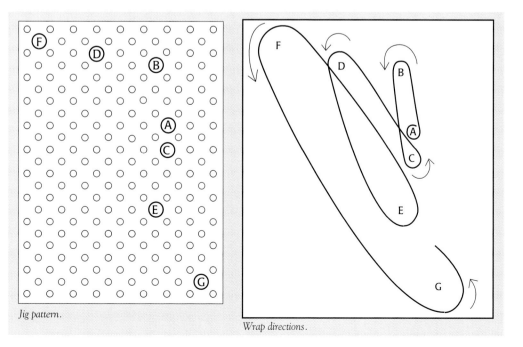

Jig pattern.

Wrap directions.

Wine Goblets

Designed by Elaine Schmidt

Make any dinner special with these unique wire-wrapped wine goblets!

You Will Need
◎ 20 gauge wire, Copper
◎ 6 round glass beads, 1/4" wide, green
◎ 2 glass wine goblets
◎ Jig and pegs
◎ Round Nose Pliers
◎ Wire Cutter

1 Create an anchor loop at one end of the wire.

2 Continue to use the round nose pliers and bend the wire after the anchor loop, creating a freeform design.

3 Hook the anchor loop on the rim of the wine goblet, then continue to bend the wire into a design. Press the design against the goblet, forcing it to take the shape of the goblet. Make it curve upwards toward the rim again and bend one of the loops over the rim, creating a hook. To add beads to the design, bring the straight end of the wire through the bead and slide the bead up to the last loop made. Then continue bending the wire as before.

4 Continue to circle around the goblet, creating a path toward the stem. Circle some of the looped wire design around the top of the stem, then wrap straight wire around the rest of the stem. When you reach the bottom of the stem, cut off the excess wire. Slide a bead over the new end and create an anchor loop after the bead.

5 Place the jig over the jig pattern, lining up the holes of the jig with the circles on the pattern. Place a small peg at each position.

6 Create an anchor loop at one end of the excess wire.

7 Slip the anchor loop onto peg A. Bring the wire around the outside of peg B with your fingers. Continue around the outside of the remaining pegs.

8 Lift the shape off of the jig and reposition the last loop of wire onto peg A, then continue wrapping more of the wire around the other pegs. Lift the shape off of the jig and force the shape into a circle, around the base of the wine goblet. You may need to return the shape to the jig and create additional loops. When the circle of loops fits around the base of the goblet, cut off the excess wire and create an anchor loop at the end.

9 Hook one anchor loop onto the other, securing the wire circle around the base of the goblet.

10 Repeat Steps 1 to 9 for the remaining goblet.

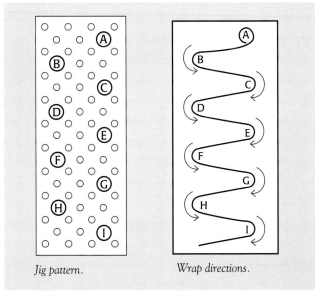

Jig pattern.　　　*Wrap directions.*

Fleur de lis Bottle

Designed by Lauren Johnston

"Simple" best describes this embellished bottle, but think of how elegant it will look filled with colored water, candy, marbles, or other small items.

You Will Need

- 18 gauge wire, Red and Gold
- Jig and pegs
- 6 glass beads, red, in various sizes
- Round Nose Pliers
- Flat Nose Pliers
- Nylon Jaw Pliers
- Wire Cutter
- Glass bottle

1 Place the jig over the jig pattern, lining up the holes of the jig with the circles on the pattern. Place a small peg at each position.

2 For the large fleur de lis (the wrap around the bottle), use jig pattern A. Make an anchor loop at one end of the wire and place onto peg A. Wrap around the pegs following the wrap directions. Remove from the pegs, then place one of the end loops back on the end peg and make another design; leave 1/2" of wire remaining in the center of the design and turn a loop (a bead will be attached to this loop). Remove from jig. Make enough of these designs to wrap around your bottle. **Note:** You may also want to make some single fleur de lis designs to insert between the double designs. When you have enough to fit around the bottle, attach together with gold wire jump rings.

3 Attach decorative beads to the wire design around the bottle with small pieces of wire (make an anchor loop on each side of the bead). Attach at the loop points or the center loop of the double fleur de lis design.

4 Slip the wire design over the bottle so that it fits snugly.

5 Make enough four-loop designs following jig pattern B to fit around the neck of the bottle. Attach the designs together with gold jump rings and slip over the top of the bottle.

6 Wrap red wire several times around the neck of the bottle.

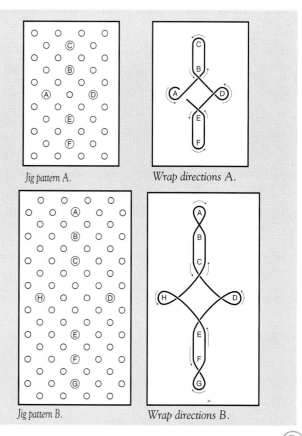

Jig pattern A.

Wrap directions A.

Jig pattern B.

Wrap directions B.

Project 46 Flatware

Ordinary flatware can get some much-needed pizzazz with two colors of wrapped wire.

You Will Need

- 22 gauge wire, Black and Silver
- 4 beads, 1/4" wide, green
- Set of flatware
- Jig and pegs
- Round Nose Pliers
- Wire Cutter

1. Make a 5/16" wide spiral at one end of one color of wire.

2. Hold the spiral at the base of the utensil handle and begin to wrap the wire around the entire length of the handle.

3. Make a spiral at one end of the other color of wire. Hold the new spiral below the first spiral, then wrap the new wire around the handle.

4. Wrap the two lengths of wire tightly around the bottom of the handle. **Note:** In the utensils shown, there is a small hole at the base of the handle and the two pieces of wire were brought through this hole. If your utensils do not have this feature, just wrap the wire tightly to secure.

5. Cut each piece of wire at the base of the handle to 1". Reserve the excess wire for later use.

6. With round nose pliers, create a loop at the middle of each wire, at the base of the handle. Use the pliers to coil the end of the wire around the top of the loop.

7. With one piece of excess wire (from Step 5), make a spiral at one end. Measure 1-1/4" after the spiral and cut off the excess wire. With pliers, make a double loop at the new end.

8. Hook the double loop of the spiral onto one of the loops at the base of the handle.

9. Place the jig over the jig pattern, lining up the holes of the jig with the circles on the pattern. Place a small peg at each position.

10. Make an anchor loop at one end of the other color of excess wire. Bring the straight end of the wire through a bead.

11 Slip the anchor loop onto peg A. The bead should fit between pegs A and B. If your bead is too large, adjust the pegs to fit. Bring the wire around peg B twice, circling that peg completely.

12 Bring the wire around the outside of peg C, circle completely around peg A, then bring the wire around the outside of peg D. To complete the shape, circle the wire around peg B. Lift the shape off the jig, cut off the excess wire, and tighten the final loop.

13 When you lift the shape off of the jig, you will notice how the loops formed at pegs A and B tend to separate. To keep the loops made on peg A together, twist the anchor loop and hook it onto the other loop.

14 Cut a 2-1/2" piece of wire using the excess wire from Step 12. Create a double loop at each end of the wire. With round nose pliers, bend the wire between the double loops to create a design. Hook one set of double loops onto the beaded shape. Hook the other set of double loops to the other loop at the base of the handle.

15 Repeat Step 1-14 for each remaining utensil.

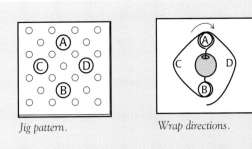

Jig pattern. *Wrap directions.*

Making a Double Loop

To make a double loop, make a basic loop on the pliers, then grip the first loop tightly. Turn the wire around the nose of the pliers a second time, creating a second loop.

Other Place Setting Ideas

◎ Find flatware with open sections on the handle and add wire and beads to fill in the opening.

◎ Wrap wire around a wine goblet and hang spiraled eye pins from the wire.

◎ Use the Be-Dazzler to add studs to a placemat and napkin.

◎ Stitch a double coil bead onto one corner of a napkin.

Candleholder

This decorative wire design can fit around any size of candle or glass candleholder.

You Will Need
- 22 gauge wire, Light Blue or Lavender
- Candle, blue or purple
- Jig and pegs
- Round Nose Pliers
- Wire Cutter

1 Place the jig over the jig pattern, lining up the holes of the jig with the circles on the pattern. Place a small peg at each position.

2 Create an anchor loop at one end of the wire. Slip the anchor loop onto peg A.

3 Bring the wire around peg B with your fingers. As you do this, loop the wire tightly around, pushing it down to the base of the peg. Continue wrapping wire around the remaining pegs.

4 Lift the shape off of the jig and reposition the loop of wire made on peg E onto peg A.

5 Repeat Steps 3 and 4 five more times. Lift the shape off of the jig, cut off the excess wire, and tighten the final loop.

6 Attach the anchor loop of the shape to the final loop made. Put the design around the candle.

7 **Optional:** Be creative and add more wire designs to the candle, as shown on the example at left.

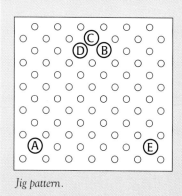

Jig pattern.

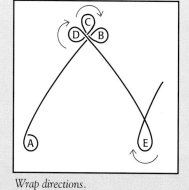

Wrap directions.

Caution!
The candles shown here have been lit for photographic purposes. Do not burn a candle with wire around it; the wire is intended for decorative use only.

Vase

Dangling wire decorations add flair to an otherwise plain vase.

You Will Need

◎ 18 gauge wire, Bare (silver)
◎ 6 round beads, 1/4" and 3/8" wide (3 of each), green
◎ Vase, blue
◎ Jig and pegs
◎ Bent Chain Nose Pliers
◎ Round Nose Pliers
◎ Nylon Jaw Pliers
◎ Wire Cutter

1 Place the jig over the jig pattern, lining up the holes of the jig with the circles on the pattern. Place a small peg at each position.

2 Cut 1 yard of wire. Make an anchor loop at one end.

3 Slip the anchor loop onto peg A. Bring the wire around the outside of peg B. Continue to wrap the wire around the rest of the pegs.

4 Lift the shape off of the jig. Reposition the shape on the jig, slipping the last loop made onto peg A. Continue to wrap the wire around the rest of the pegs.

5 Repeat Step 4 a few more times, creating a long continuous curve of loops. Make the curve long enough to circle around the vase. Cut off the excess wire and tighten the last loop. Connect the last loop to the first loop, closing the circle.

6 Cut about 12" of wire for each hanging decoration. Make a double loop at one end of each 12" piece of wire. Use bent chain nose pliers to create bends in each piece of wire.

7 Slip a bead onto the wire, then measure 2" after the bead and cut off the excess wire at that point. Make a loose spiral after the bead.

8 Hook the double loop of each beaded wire shape onto the loops of the wire circle.

9 Put the wire decoration around the vase.

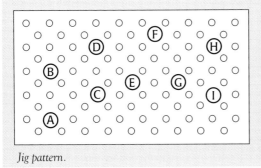

Jig pattern.

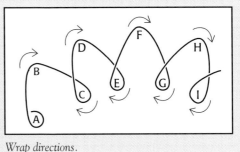

Wrap directions.

Bubble Wands

Designed by Lauren Johnston

Who doesn't love blowing bubbles on a beautiful summer day? Now you can make your own stylish versions that ensure hours of fun!

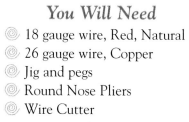

You Will Need

- 18 gauge wire, Red, Natural
- 26 gauge wire, Copper
- Jig and pegs
- Round Nose Pliers
- Wire Cutter

Use the heart, star, or flower jig pattern to insert pegs into the jig. Place the jig over the pattern, lining up the holes of the jig with the circles on the pattern. Place a small peg at each position.

Flower

You will need approximately 24" of 18 gauge natural wire. Make an anchor loop and slip it onto peg A. Follow the wrap directions to create the flower. Leave the extra wire attached and remove from the pegs. Twist the extra end piece of wire around the loop point where you started.

Heart

You will need approximately 24" of 18 gauge red wire. Leave about 7" of wire at one end, then follow the jig pattern, beginning with a loop at the bottom of the heart facing inward and ending with another loop at the other end, facing inward. Remove from the pegs and separate the two loops at the bottom so they form a bow shape. Twist the extra wire together to

make a handle and form half heart shapes at the ends using round nose pliers.

Star

You will need approximately 24" of 18 gauge copper wire. Leave about 6" to 7" of wire at one end, then follow the jig pattern, beginning with a loop at the bottom of the star facing inward. Leave the extra wire attached and remove from the pegs. Twist the extra end piece of wire around the loop point where you started. Twist the extra wire together to make a handle and form coil shapes at the ends using round nose pliers.

Finishing All

Determine how long you want the handle (5-1/2" is shown) and bend the wire back onto itself; trim off excess. Wrap the entire handle with 26 gauge copper wire.

Jig pattern (flower).

Jig pattern (heart).

Jig pattern (star).

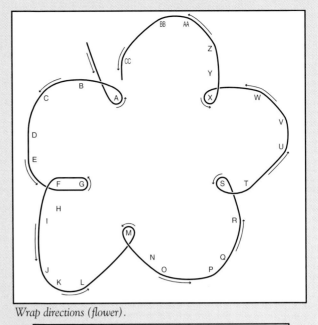

Wrap directions (flower).

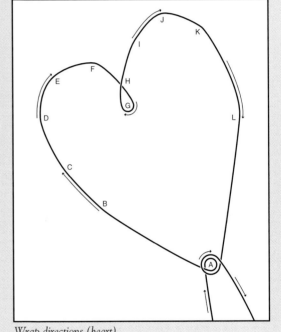

Wrap directions (heart).

Wrap directions (star).

Doggy Bone Frame

Designed by Lauren Johnston

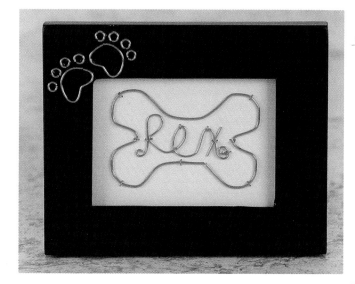

Immortalize your favorite pet with its own frame!

You Will Need

- 18 gauge wire, Natural
- 20 and 26 gauge wire, Tinned Copper
- Jig and pegs
- Cardstock, cream
- Round Nose Pliers
- Flat Nose Pliers
- Nylon Jaw Pliers
- Wire Cutter
- Small frame with flat front
- Needle tool and small piece of craft foam
- Glue

1 Place the jig over jig pattern A, lining up the holes of the jig with the circles on the pattern. Place a small peg at each position. Follow the pattern with the natural wire; slide off of the jig and cut excess wire.

2 Cut the cardstock to fit in the opening of the frame.

3 Attach the dog bone to piece of cardstock by making tiny holes with the needle tool (place on foam cushion to do this) around each letter. Make 1/2" horseshoe shapes with the 26 gauge tinned copper wire. Insert these horseshoe shapes through the tiny holes around the letters and secure by flattening the wire at the back of the cardstock.

4 Make the desired wire letters with 20 gauge tinned copper wire and round nose pliers. Attach to the center of the bone as in Step 3.

5 Make eight jump rings with 20 gauge tinned copper wire.

6 Place the jig over jig pattern B, lining up the holes of the jig with the circles on the pattern. Place a small peg at B and C and a small peg at A. Follow the pattern with the 20 gauge tinned copper wire; slide off of the jig and make a slight indentation in the bottom of the paw with round nose pliers. Cut excess wire.

7 Glue the paws, with jump rings as "claws," onto the front of the frame, in the upper left corner.

8 Put cardstock into the frame.

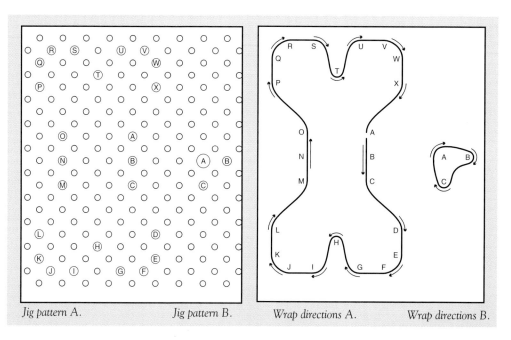

Jig pattern A.　　　Jig pattern B.　　　Wrap directions A.　　　Wrap directions B.

Ringlet Frame

Designed by Lauren Johnston

What could be easier than creating rings to attach to a frame? The results are stunning!

You Will Need

◎ 20 gauge wire, Magenta and Tinned Copper
◎ Twist n' Curl and large metal and plastic rods
◎ Round Nose Pliers
◎ Flat Nose Pliers
◎ Nylon Jaw Pliers
◎ Wire Cutter
◎ Frame with flat front
◎ Glue
◎ Photograph

1 Assemble the Twist n' Curl with the large metal rod for the Tinned Copper rings and the large round plastic rod for the Magenta rings. Twist approximately 3" of coils on each size rod.

2 Slide each coil off of the rod.

3 Cut each ring from the coil one at a time, exactly at the location of the cut of the previous ring. Continue through the entire coil until all of the rings are formed.

4 To finish, flatten the two ends of each wire ring together using the nylon jaw pliers.

5 Squeeze glue onto the frame where you want the designs; lay on a magenta jump ring, then a tinned copper jump ring on the inside. Continue until the entire frame is covered. Allow to dry.

Making Jump Rings

The process described in Steps 1 to 3 are very effective for making large quantities of jump rings. Follow this procedure for any of the projects in this book that require multiple jump rings.

Gift Box

This decorative lid can be adjusted to fit any size box by changing the size or number of beads or the amount of wire used and the size of the wire shapes.

You Will Need

- 22 gauge wire, Copper
- 4" square gift box
- 24 square beads, 7/16" long, red
- Jig and pegs
- Round Nose Pliers
- Wire Cutter

1 Place the jig over the jig pattern, lining up the holes of the jig with the circles on the pattern. Place a small peg at each position.

2 Cut a 28" piece of wire and create an anchor loop at one end.

3 Slip the anchor loop onto peg A. Bring the wire around peg B with your fingers. As you do this, loop the wire tightly around, pushing it down to the base of the peg. Continue wrapping wire around the remaining pegs. Do not wrap the wire around peg J.

4 Lift the shape off of the jig and reposition the loop of wire made on peg I onto peg A. Continue wrapping the length of wire around pegs C through I again. Continue to lift the shape off the jig and reposition the last loop onto peg A until you have created 11 loops on one side of the shape and 12 loops on the other side.

5 Lift the shape off of the jig and reposition the last two loops onto pegs H and I. Wrap the wire around peg J to complete the shape. Lift the shape off of the jig and check that the length of the wire shape fits across the top of the box. If necessary, adjust the amount of loops to fit the size of the box. Cut off the excess wire and tighten the final loop.

6 Repeat Steps 1 to 5 until you have a total of seven wire shapes.

7 Cut a 2" piece of wire, make an anchor loop at the end, slide on one bead, and make another loop after the bead, making a simple bead link. Repeat until you have a total of 24 bead links.

8 With the remaining wire, create 42 wire jump rings.

9 To assemble the top of the decorative lid, connect the wire shapes together with the bead links. To do this, locate the anchor loop of one of the wire shapes. Lay the shape down so that the anchor loop is at the top right. Connect a bead link to every loop along the right side of the wire shape.

10 Attach the other side of the bead links to another wire shape. This time, position the wire shape so that the anchor loop is at top left. Add another row of bead links and attach a third wire shape. At this point, check that the width of the decorative top fits across the box. The wire shapes can be manipulated a little to make it fit.

11 Attach a wire shape to each side of the lid with wire jump rings. Once all four sides are attached, close the corners of the lid by attaching a jump ring to the top and bottom corner of each side panel.

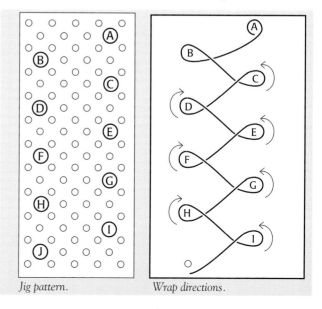

Jig pattern.   Wrap directions.

Wired Mobile

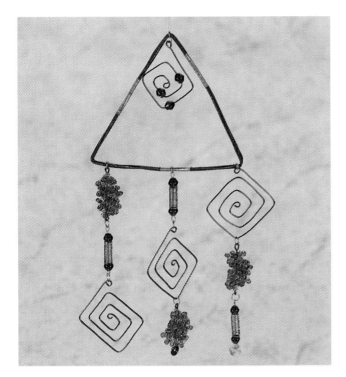

Think mobiles are child's play? Think again! This unique design will look great hanging in a window or from a light fixture or ceiling fan.

You Will Need

- 18 and 26 gauge wire, Green
- 20 and 24 gauge wire, Tinned Copper
- Twist n' Curl and small and large metal rods
- Decorative glass beads, small and large, green
- Round Nose Pliers
- Flat Nose Pliers
- Nylon Jaw Pliers
- Wire Cutter
- Monofilament thread
- Transparent tape

1 For the beaded baubles, assemble the Twist n' Curl using the small metal rod. Using 24 gauge tinned copper and approximately 48 small decorative green beads, twist a coil about 3-1/2" long. Twist one or two times between the insertions of each bead. Make three beaded baubles.

2 Use an additional piece of 24 gauge tinned copper wire and the Twist n' Curl to form a double coil bead, again with the small metal rod. Insert a separate piece of 18 gauge wire through the center and turn a loop for the ones that need to be attached to other hanging items. Form a flat coil with round nose pliers for the one hanging at the bottom of the mobile.

3 Make three square spirals, each about 2" wide, using 18 gauge green wire. Begin each with a loop and end with a loop.

4 Make an additional square spiral, about 1-1/2" wide, for the center of the triangle, threading on large green beads where desired.

5 For the long tinned copper beads, assemble the Twist n' Curl using the large metal rod. Use 20 gauge tinned copper and make a coil approximately

3" long; cut this into three pieces of equal length. Insert a separate piece of 20 gauge wire through the center of each bead. Add a large decorative green bead at each end and turn a loop for the ones that need to be attached to other hanging items. Form a spiral for the one hanging at the bottom of the mobile.

6 Make 10 wire jump rings with tinned copper wire.

7 For the triangle, cut a piece of 18 gauge green wire 13-1/2" long and bend at 4-1/2" intervals. Make three of these and hold together with small pieces of tape, alternating where the cut edges meet.

8 Alternate wrapping this triangle with 24 gauge tinned copper and 26 gauge green wire until it is completely covered.

9 Assemble the dangling pieces and attach with jump rings. Attach these pieces to the wired triangle with additional jump rings.

10 Attach the dangling piece in the top of the triangle with jump rings and secure with monofilament thread to hang the mobile.

Section 3
Projects for Giving and Preserving Memories

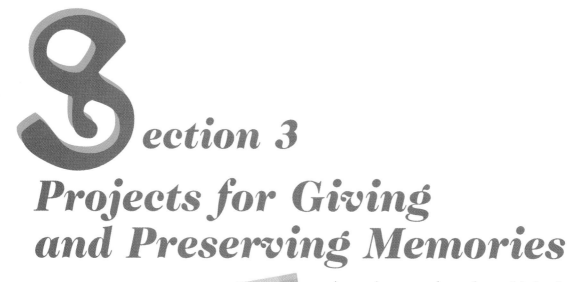

As you've seen throughout this book, wire can add new dimensions to a wide variety of projects. Why not take advantage of wire's unique characteristics and add life to otherwise flat paper items? Here you will discover how to shape coils into birthday candles and garland and turn ordinary spirals into extraordinary flowers, grapes, and even cheery holly berries. Once discover how easy it is, you'll be hooked! Note: It is recommended to store wire-embellished scrapbook pages in plastic page protectors.

irthday Candles Card

Designed by Valoree Albert

Springy coiled candles are a fun way to wish someone a happy birthday!

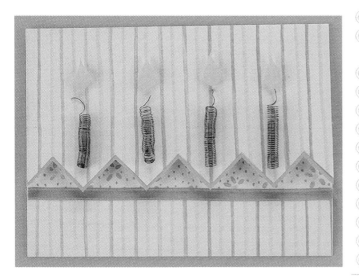

You Will Need

- 22 gauge wire, Peacock Blue
- 12" x 6-1/2" piece of cardstock, blue and yellow striped
- 6-1/2" x 3-1/2" piece of cardstock, blue
- 6-1/2" x 2-1/2" piece of cardstock, floral
- Scrap of cardstock, yellow
- Pop dots
- 6-1/2" of 1/4" wide satin ribbon, blue
- Scissors
- Glue
- Ruler and scoring tool
- Permanent marker, black
- Twist n' Curl and small metal rod
- Wire Cutter

1 With the ruler and scoring tool, score a line 3-1/2" in from one end and 4" in from the other end of the blue and yellow striped cardstock. Fold on the score lines, forming a tri-fold card.

2 On 3-1/2" folded section, cut away five triangles, each about 3/4" deep.

3 Glue the blue cardstock to the back of the 3-1/2" section with the cut-away triangles. Cut the blue cardstock following the shape of triangles of the striped cardstock, leaving about 1/8" of the blue showing.

4 On the front of the 4" end of striped cardstock, attach the floral cardstock. Glue the ribbon over the join of the striped and floral cardstocks. Close the card; you should see the points of the triangles just touching the ribbon just placed; the floral cardstock should be visible through the triangle openings.

5 With the Twist n' Curl and small metal rod make four wire coils; the coils should be about 1-1/2" long, with a 1/2" tail piece of wire left at one end.

6 Glue the wire coils to the front of the card, in the indents of the four triangle points. The 1/2" tails of wire, which serve as the candle wicks, should be pointing up.

7 Cut four small flames from the scrap of yellow cardstock. Attach a pop dot to the back of each flame and add a flame above each candle.

8 Write a message inside of the card.

Thanks a Whole Bunch Card

Designed by Valoree Albert

This heartfelt card will be appreciated by the recipient.

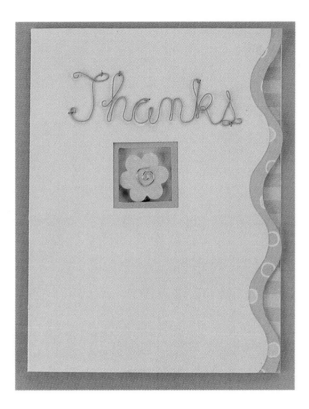

You Will Need

- 22 gauge wire, Light and Dark Green
- 22 gauge wire, scraps of Copper, Plum, Peacock Blue, Magenta, Bare (silver)
- 10" x 6-1/2" piece of cardstock, white
- 5" x 6-1/2" piece of cardstock, green dotted
- 3/4" x 6-1/2" piece of cardstock, pink and yellow striped
- Cardstock scraps, purple, yellow, pink, blue, silver
- 2" x 2" piece of cardstock, light and dark brown
- Raffia, green
- Pop dots
- Scissors
- Permanent marker, black
- X-acto knife, ruler, cutting mat
- Glue
- Wire Writer
- Jig and pegs
- Round Nose Pliers
- Nylon Jaw Pliers
- Wire Cutter

1 Fold the white cardstock in half, making it 5" x 6-1/2". One on 6-1/2" side, the card front, cut a wavy line; the "dips" should be about 3/4" deep.

2 Lay the cardstock flat on the cutting mat. Cut a 1-1/4" square out of the front, about 2-1/4" down from the top and 1-3/4" in from the left side.

3 Glue the green dotted cardstock on the inside of the card's front. Cut a wavy line in the green cardstock that outlines the white lines. Leave about 1/4" of green cardstock showing.

4 Cut away the green cardstock in the opening from Step 2, leaving about 1/8" showing.

5 Cut a wavy line in one side of the striped cardstock. Glue this to the inside of the card, along the right edge.

6 Place the jig over the jig pattern, lining up the holes of the jig with the circles on the pattern. Place a small peg at each position. Using the Wire Writer and light green wire, follow the jig pattern to write "Thanks." When you are done, attach the letters to the front of the card with small pieces of wire. Place "Thanks" above the opening.

7 Write a message inside of the card, near the top.

8 Cut the brown cardstock, light and dark, into 1/4" wide strips. Weave the cardstock together and carefully glue it together. Cut the cardstock into the shape of a vase or basket. Wrap two pieces of bare wire around the vase.

9 Cut four flowers from the scraps of cardstock. Create four small spirals and glue one to the

middle of each corresponding color of flower.

10 Using the dark green wire and the Twist n' Curl with the small metal rod, make four coils, varying in length from 2" to 3" long once stretched.

11 Cut small pieces of raffia. Glue the raffia and the ends of the four wire coils to the back of the vase. You can bend and shape the coils to look like flower stems.

12 Attach pop dots to the back of the vase and attach it to the inside of the card, near the bottom.

13 Position the wires so that one flower will appear through the window in the front of the card. Using pop dots, attach the flowers to the inside of the card, one above each wire stem.

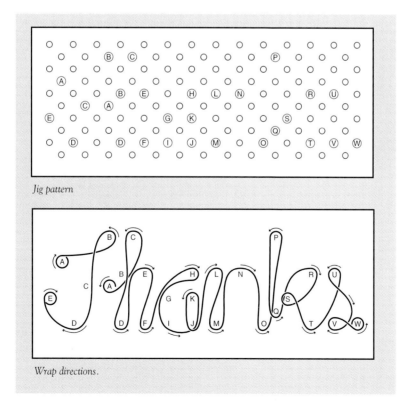

Jig pattern

Wrap directions.

56 Be-Dazzled Flower Card

Designed by Elaine Schmidt

The combination of studs, jigged wire, and spiral "leaves" make this an interesting card that can be used for a number of occasions.

You Will Need

- 20 gauge wire, Plum and Dark Green
- 10" x 7" piece of cardstock, magenta
- 4" x 6" piece of cardstock, black
- 3-1/2" x 5-1/2" piece of cardstock, bright green
- 1 stud, gold
- 6 small round studs, green
- Glue
- Jig and pegs
- Rounds Nose Pliers
- Nylon Jaw Pliers
- Wire Cutter
- Custom Hand Tool

1 Fold the magenta cardstock in half so it measures 5" x 7".

2 Position the gold stud on the bright green cardstock, about 1-1/2" down from the top and in the center. Push the stud through the cardstock and use the Custom Hand Tool to flatten the prongs against the back of the cardstock.

3 Position the six green studs below the gold stud, starting about 1/2" from the gold stud. Leave about 1/2" between each stud. Again push the studs through the cardstock and use the Custom Hand Tool to flatten the prongs against the back of the cardstock.

4 Place the jig over the jig pattern, lining up the holes of the jig with the circles on the pattern. Place a small peg at each position. Using purple wire, create the flower design. Leave about 1/2" at both ends of the wire to attach the design to the green cardstock. Push the 1/2" ends into the cardstock, around the gold stud.

5 Make two spirals, each about 1/2" in diameter. Leave about 3/4" at the end of the wire to attach the spirals to the green cardstock. Poke the wire into the cardstock for leaves, between the third and fourth and fourth and fifth green studs.

6 Glue the green cardstock to the center of the black cardstock.

7 Choose one side of the magenta cardstock as the front of the card. Glue the black cardstock to the center of the magenta cardstock's front.

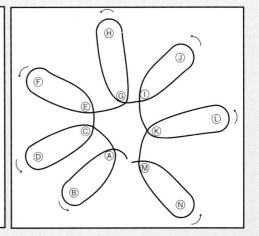

Jig pattern　　　　*Wrap directions.*

Birth Announcement Card

Designed by Valoree Albert

This sweet little card is the perfect way for a proud mother and father to announce the arrival of their precious baby.

You Will Need

- 24 gauge wire, Magenta and Bare (silver)
- 6-1/2" x 10" piece of cardstock, white
- 5" x 6-1/2" piece of vellum, white
- 5-1/2" x 4" piece of cardstock, printed with baby sayings and animals*
- 16" of 1/4" wide satin ribbon, pink
- Pop dots
- Scissors
- Glue
- Permanent marker, black
- Transparent tape
- Twist n' Curl
- Round Nose Pliers
- Wire Cutter

*You will also need a scrap of this cardstock to be used for the closures of the pins.

1 Fold the white cardstock in half so it measures 5" x 6-1/2".

2 Choose one side of the folded cardstock as the front. Glue the printed cardstock to the center of the card front.

3 Glue the vellum to the card front, over the printed cardstock.

4 Cut four rounded pieces of paper from the scrap of printed cardstock. Try to center an animal in each piece. These pieces will serve as the pin closures.

5 Using round nose pliers, form the four safety pins, each with a 4" piece of wire. Create one loop near the middle of the wire and bend the ends to form a "U" shape. Poke each wire into the front of the card, through the vellum and printed cardstock. Put the first pin about 1" in from the left side of the card and

about 1-1/4" up from the bottom. Leave about 1/2" between each pin. If desired, put small pieces of transparent tape over the wire ends on the back of the card.

6 Attach a pop dot to the back of each pin closure. Position one pin closure above each pin wire.

7 Wrap and glue the pink ribbon around the card front, near the fold. Cut off the excess and make a small bow.

8 Using pliers, make a freeform wire design, about 5-1/2" long. Glue the middle of the wire to the middle of the ribbon. Glue the bow made in Step 7 to the middle of the wire and ribbon.

9 Write a message on the inside of the card.

Oh, Christmas Tree Card

Send holiday cheer to your loved ones with this festive card.

You Will Need
- 24 gauge wire, Bare (silver)
- 1 small heart stud, silver
- 6-1/2" x 11" piece of cardstock, green
- 5" x 6" piece of foil paper, silver
- 4-1/2" x 5-1/2" piece of cardstock, red
- 4-1/2" x 4" tree die-cut, green
- Glue
- Transparent tape
- Permanent marker, black
- Twist n' Curl and medium round rod
- Wire Cutter
- Custom Hand Tool

1 Glue the tree die-cut to the red cardstock, about 3/4" from the top edge.

2 Using the Twist n' Curl and bare wire, make one long loose single coil, approximately 1 foot long.

3 Cut the coil into seven lengths to "wrap" back and forth across the tree to act as garland. Starting at the top of the tree, poke one end of the shortest piece of wire into the cardstock; position the wire and poke the other end into the cardstock. Smooth the wire ends to the back of the cardstock and cover with small pieces of transparent tape.

4 Repeat Step 3 with the remaining pieces of wire, zigzagging the wire across the tree and working toward the base.

5 Carefully push the prongs of the star stud through the red cardstock, just above the tree die-cut. Using the Custom Hand Tool, curve and smooth the prongs to the back of the cardstock. Attach a piece of transparent tape over the prongs, if desired.

6 Glue the red cardstock to the center of the silver foil paper.

7 Fold the green cardstock in half, so that the dimensions are 5-1/2" x 6-1/2". Glue the silver foil paper to the center of the green cardstock's front.

8 Write a message on the inside of the card.

Celebrate Card

Designed by Valoree Albert

Wish your friends and relatives a happy and safe New Year with this eye-catching card. Wouldn't this make a great party invitation?

You Will Need

- 22 gauge wire, Red, Bare (silver), Peacock Blue, Dark Blue
- 1 ft. of 1/4" wide paper ribbon, silver
- 6-1/4" square piece of cardstock, diamond pattern
- 5" square piece of vellum, white
- Permanent marker, black
- Glue
- Transparent tape
- Twist n' Curl and small metal rod
- Nylon Jaw Pliers
- Wire Cutter

1. Write a message on the vellum, starting about 1-1/2" from the left side.

2. Apply glue to the four corners of the vellum. Adhere the vellum to the cardstock, directly in the center.

3. Cut three 1-1/2" pieces of blue wire. Create a spiral with each piece, leaving about 1/2" uncurled. Pierce one spiral into each corner of the vellum (except the upper left, where the arrangement made in Step 5 will go) through the cardstock. Smooth the excess 1/2" to the back of the cardstock and cover with a small piece of transparent tape.

4. Using the Twist n' Curl, make six loose single coils, each about 3" to 3-1/2" long; make two from dark blue, two from bare, one from peacock blue, and one from red.

5. Gather the wire coils in a bundle and tie the silver ribbon around them into a bow.

6. Carefully apply glue to the back of the ribbon and attach the arrangement to the upper left portion of the vellum.

Love Card

Rubber-stamped hearts form the perfect background for a layered craft foam heart on this "lovely" card.

You Will Need

- 22 gauge wire, Red and Bare (silver)
- Craft foam, pink and black
- 3 small heart studs, silver
- 10" x 7" piece of cardstock, red
- Dye inkpads, dark pink and purple
- Heart rubber stamp
- 1/8" hole punch
- Pop dots
- Glue
- Scissors
- Custom Hand Tool
- Nylon Jaw Pliers
- Wire Writer, Jig, pegs

1 Fold the piece of cardstock in half so that it measures 5" x 7".

2 Randomly stamp the heart onto the front of the card; use both the dark pink and purple inks. Allow to dry.

3 Using the pattern provided, cut out the larger heart outline from the black craft foam. Cut out smaller heart outline from the pink craft foam.

4 Place the jig over the jig pattern, lining up the holes of the jig with the circles on the pattern. Place a small peg at each position. Using the jig pattern, Wire Writer, and red wire, write "Love," beginning and ending with a spiral. Using small pieces of wire, attach "Love" to the pink heart, at an angle.

5 Randomly place the three heart studs on the pink heart. Use the Custom Hand Tool to bend and smooth the prongs to the back of the foam.

6 Glue the pink heart on top of the black heart.

7 Punch three small holes into the black foam, near the bottom, one directly under the "point" of the pink heart and one on either side.

8 Create three small spirals with bare wire, each about 3/4" long. Attach these spirals to the black heart, in the holes made in Step 7. Bend the wire around the openings with pliers.

9 Using pop dots, attach the heart ensemble to the front of the card, at an angle.

Cut small heart from pink craft foam.

Cut large heart from black craft foam.

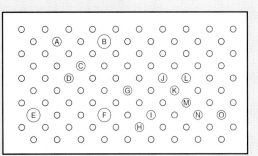

Jig pattern

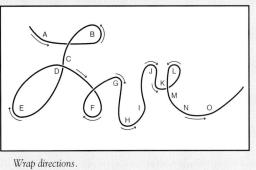

Wrap directions.

Try reducing the heart patterns and making a pin. Simply follow the instructions for assembling the layered hearts and glue on a pin back.

If Friends Were Flowers... Card

Designed by Valoree Albert

Breezy white vellum and wood-patterned paper make this window card one the recipient will cherish.

You Will Need

- 24 gauge wire, Plum
- 6 metallic leaves, green
- 10" x 6-1/2" piece of cardstock, white
- 4-3/4" x 4" piece of vellum, white
- 5-1/2" x 1-1/4" piece of cardstock, wood pattern
- Glue
- Permanent marker, black
- Pencil
- Scissors
- X-acto knife, cutting mat, ruler
- Pop dots
- Round Nose Pliers
- Nylon Jaw Pliers
- Wire Cutter

1 Fold the piece of white cardstock in half to measure 5" x 6-1/2".

2 Choose one side as the front. Cut away a rectangle that measures 5" x 2-1/4" from the bottom of the front.

3 Open the card. On the front, mark four window openings, each approximately 1-3/4" x 1-1/2". Use the cutting mat, X-acto knife, and ruler to cut away the windows openings.

4 Carefully apply glue to the back of the window-pane (on the inside of the card) and adhere the vellum.

5 Write a message on the inside of the card.

6 Cut away a small section on each end of the wood-patterned cardstock to resemble a window box; the bottom edge of the window box should be 5" long. Using pop dots, attach the window box to the card, below the window opening.

7 Make approximately 15 spirals with the plum wire, each about 1/2" wide.

8 Glue the spirals in a random fashion above the window box. Because the window box is elevated, you can tuck some of the spiral "flowers" behind the box.

9 Randomly glue the six leaves amongst the flowers.

Grape Bunch Journal

Simple wire spirals make up the grapes on this unique journal cover.

You Will Need
- 20 gauge wire, Red and Dark Green
- 10" piece of 3/4" wide sheer satin ribbon, green
- 7" x 5" spiral-bound journal, natural
- Tacky glue
- Round Nose Pliers
- Nylon Jaw Pliers
- Wire Cutter

1 Using the red wire, create approximately 19 spirals, ranging in diameter from 5/16" to 1/2".

2 Make the "stem" with green wire. Cut a piece of wire about 1 foot long. Make a spiral at one end and freeform a curved design with the round nose pliers. Make a spiral on the other end.

3 Glue the stem onto the journal cover at an angle, near the upper right-hand corner.

4 Now randomly glue the red spirals made in Step 1 to the journal cover, forming a bunch of grapes beneath the stem.

5 Make a bow with the piece of ribbon. Glue the knot to the stem.

Other Journal Ideas
- Use studs or rhinestones as the centers of flowers.
- Write your name or a special message with the Wire Writer and jig and attach to the cover.
- Make coiled wire beads and hang them from the spiral binding.

Sugar and Spice... Scrapbook Page

Designed by Valoree Albert

Use wire to decorate a page that commemorates a special dress-up party.

You Will Need

- 22 gauge wire, Pink and Bare (silver)
- 12" square scrapbook paper, white with pink flowers
- 12" x 3" piece of scrapbook paper, pink checked
- Scrapbook paper, green, cut to size to matte photographs
- Vellum, white
- 2" x 4" piece of scrapbook paper, silver
- Seed beads, pink
- Small amount of confetti, pink
- Glitter, pink
- Acid-free glue
- Acid-free marker, black
- Scissors
- 2 photographs
- Round Nose Pliers
- Wire Cutter

1 On one side of the white scrapbook paper, carefully tear away about 1-1/2".

2 Matte the two photographs with green paper. Write the names of the people in the photograph on vellum; cut out and adhere to the photographs. Position the matted photographs on the white paper, one near the upper right corner and one angled along the left side.

3 Write a message on the vellum. For the word "sugar," glue was applied in the open spaces in the letters and glitter added. Attach the vellum to the white paper; "Sugar" and "and" should be at upper left and the longer message at lower right.

4 Write "Spice" on the silver paper; cut out. Cut a piece of vellum large enough to fit under the word. Attach some confetti to the vellum and then attach "Spice" to it. Attach the vellum to the white paper, under "Sugar."

5 Make a three-sided wire frame for the upper left-hand corner. To do this, use round nose pliers to create twists and loops in the pink wire. Attach the wire to the paper with small pieces of wire.

6 Place the jig over the flower jig pattern on page 85, lining up the holes of the jig with the circles on the pattern. Place a small peg at each position. Use the jig pattern to make a large flower with the pink wire. Attach this flower to the white paper with small pieces of wire, between the lower picture and vellum message.

7 Cut a piece of wire that is approximately 15" long. Make a couple of anchor loops at one end. String seed beads onto the wire. As you are stringing beads, carefully make some loops in the wire. After you have strung beads the length of the wire, create additional anchor loops on the other end. Attach this beaded wire to the pink checked paper with small pieces of wire.

8 Turn the white paper over. Adhere the small checked piece of paper to the back of the white paper so that the beaded wire faces the front.

Ewe Surprised Me Scrapbook Page

Designed by Valoree Albert

Here's a great way to remember a surprise party… Think of a fun play-on-words (like "Ewe Surprised Me") and follow the theme throughout the page.

You Will Need

- 20 gauge wire, Lavender, Green, Aqua, Gray
- 12" square piece of scrapbook paper, purple checked
- Scrapbook paper, purple and lavender, cut in sizes to matte the photographs
- Scrap of scrapbook paper, black
- Heavy cardstock, white
- 3 buttons, 1/4" to 3/4" in diameter, shades of purple
- 3 photographs
- 1 themed picture*
- Pop dot
- Acid-free markers, purple and white
- Acid-free glue
- Round Nose Pliers
- Nylon Jaw Pliers
- Wire Cutter

*The picture shown here is of Noah's Ark, which has been colored. Choose a picture that is appropriate for your scrapbook page and add wire to the picture as desired.

1 Matte each of the photographs with lavender paper and then with purple paper.

2 Write "Ewe Surprised Me" (or other message) and the name and date of the event on the white cardstock. Carefully tear the edges of the paper. Matte these pieces of paper with purple paper.

3 Thread purple wire through the holes in the buttons and, using round nose pliers, join the three buttons together with bends and turns of wire. Glue the joined buttons to the top left corner of the matted piece of paper with the message on it.

4 Tear the edges of the paper around the picture. Matte the picture with purple paper. Make about seven loose spirals with the green and aqua wire for waves. Glue the wire to the picture as desired.

5 To make the sheep, cut an oval (about 3/4" long) for the head, two smaller ovals for the ears, two small rectangles for the legs, and one small oval for the tail from black paper. Put two white dots on the sheep's head for eyes. Glue the two small ears to the back of the head. Using a pop dot, attach the head to a white piece of cardstock. Now glue the legs and tail onto the cardstock; from ear to tail, the sheep should be about 2-1/4" long.

6 Use gray wire to make a few loose spirals for the sheep's body. Glue the wire to the cardstock to form the body. Carefully tear the cardstock and matte the sheep with purple paper.

7 To complete the page, glue all of the components to the purple checked background paper: Put the button-embellished piece, the name and date, and the sheep across the top of the paper; below these, put two photographs; finally, add the final photograph and the matted picture.

Happy Holly Days Scrapbook Page

Designed by Valoree Albert

Use a jig to create holly leaves to add a festive touch to any holiday page.

You Will Need

- 22 gauge wire, Dark Green and Red
- 12" square piece of scrapbook paper, white
- 9-1/2" square piece of scrapbook paper, green and white checked
- Scrapbook paper, green and white, cut in sizes to matte photographs and for text
- 2 photographs
- Paper cutout or sticker, gift packages
- Computer or acid-free marker, black
- Scissors
- Acid-free glue
- Jig and pegs
- Round Nose Pliers
- Nylon Jaw Pliers

1 Glue the green checked paper to the middle of the white background paper.

2 Matte each of the photographs with the white paper. Next, matte the photographs with the green paper. Glue the photographs to the green checked paper, each at an angle.

3 Type or write your message on another piece of white paper. Cut the message out and matte with green paper. Glue the message to the green checked and background paper.

4 Attach the cutout or sticker to the green checked paper.

5 Use red wire to make four small spirals (holly berries), each about 1/4" in diameter. Glue these spirals to the corners of the matted message.

6 Place the jig over the jig pattern, lining up the holes of the jig with the circles on the pattern. Place a small peg at each position. Using the jig and green wire, make 11 holly leaves; attach the leaves to the white background paper using small pieces of wire.

7 Make 15 additional spirals with red wire, ranging from 1/4" to 1/2" in diameter. Glue these spirals to the background paper, near or between the wire holly leaves.

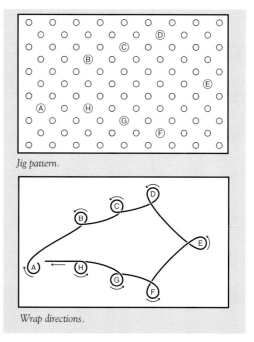

Jig pattern.

Wrap directions.

Wedding Day Scrapbook Page

Designed by Valoree Albert

This scrapbook page will always be cherished by the happy couple!

You Will Need

- 24 gauge wire, Bare (silver), Red, Green
- 12" piece of scrapbook paper, green and white striped
- 8" x 6" piece of scrapbook paper, dark green*
- 6" x 4" piece of scrapbook paper, white
- 6-1/2" x 4-1/2" and 4" x 6" pieces of vellum, white
- Tissue paper, iridescent green
- 12" of 1/4" wide ribbon, silver
- 4 reinforcement rings, silver, 1/4" hole punch
- 1 photograph
- Acid-free marker, black
- Acid-free glue
- Wire Writer
- Jig and pegs
- Round Nose Pliers
- Nylon Jaw Pliers
- Wire Cutter

*You will also need a scrap of this paper to frame the first letter of the message.

1. Matte the photograph on the white piece of paper. Now matte the photograph on the green piece of paper.

2. Using the pliers and bare wire, create a "frame" for the photograph. Make freeform loops in the wire and attach the wire to the green matte with small pieces of wire.

3. Glue the matted photograph to the green and white striped background paper, about 1/2" from the top, in the center.

4. Using the Wire Writer and jig pattern, make a "T" with the bare wire; see page 93 for the jig pattern. Attach the letter to the scrap of green paper. Cut a piece of tissue paper to matte the letter. Glue the matted letter to the 6-1/2" x 4-1/2" piece of vellum, about 1" in from the top and left side.

5. Write the rest of the message with the marker; this page says "There is no surprise more wonderful than the surprise of being loved."

6. Using the four reinforcement rings, attach the vellum message to the background paper, near the lower right corner.

7. Put a piece of tissue paper over the remaining piece of vellum; position the tissue about 2" above the vellum. Fold the vellum and tissue into a vase shape; fold the sides in and the top of the vellum outward. The tissue should serve as a liner and stick out of the top of the vellum.

8. Create six roses with the red wire. Use the Nylon Jaw Pliers to make the inner spirals and then loop extra wire around to form an oval shape.

9. To create the stems, cut a piece of green wire 3" to 4" long. Bend about 1" over and form a loop; wrap the tail around the "stem" and one rose to form a leaf shape. Tuck each stem into the "vase"; glue, if necessary, to secure.

10. Tie the ribbon in a bow and glue the knot to the vase. Glue the completed vase to the page.

Other Ideas

Here are some additional ideas for greeting cards and scrapbook pages.

Hearts that love
are always
in bloom.

I Love You!

David

Express your love with this special card!
Simply fold the sides of a large piece of cardstock to the middle and embellish the outside
flaps with wire shapes. For the inside, layer
different colors of cardstock and add wire
hearts and a freeform design. To make the
card extra special, make a gift tag which
bears the recipient's name. Designed by
Valoree Albert.

Commemorate your visit to a theme park with a personalized scrapbook page! Simply use a jig to create a wire outline of a favorite character, person, or other recognizable figure and attach it to the page with small pieces of wire. Designed by Valoree Albert.

Let's not forget the men! This masculine page mixes thin sisal rope and silver coils very effectively; the man in your life will appreciate it! Designed by Valoree Albert.

Project Index

Jewelry Sets

Project 4
Double Coil Set
Page 26

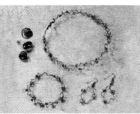

Project 11
Coiled Bead Set
Page 34

Project 12
Jewel-tone Jewelry Set
Page 36

Project 15
Twisted Loop Set
Page 40

Project 20
Wrapped Coil Set
Page 46

Project 21
Curls and Beads Set
Page 47

Project 24
Fiesta Jewelry Set
Page 50

Project 25
Figure-eight Draped Set
Page 52

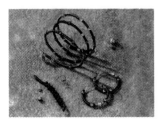

Project 27
Snake Coil Set
Page 55

Project 32
Triple Coil Set
Page 62

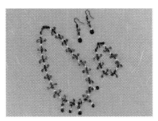

Project 33
Black Dangling Beaded Set
Page 64

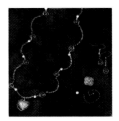

Project 34
Twisted Heart Set
Page 66

Necklaces

Project 1
Red, White, and Blue
Necklace
Page 23

Project 2
Heart Pendant Necklace
Page 24

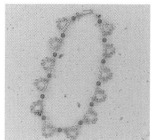

Project 6
Drop Necklace
Page 28

Project 7
Gold Filigree Necklace
Page 29

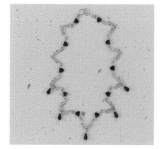

Project 8
Triangular Bead Necklace
Page 30

Project 9
Linked Necklace
Page 31

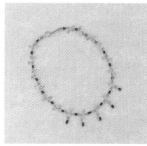

Project 13
Gold and Pink Drop
Necklace
Page 37

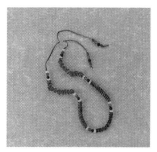

Project 22
Coils and Cord Necklace
Page 48

Project 28
Red and Silver Coil
Necklace
Page 56

Project 30
Sampler Necklace 1
Page 58

Project 31
Sampler Necklace 2
Page 60

Bracelets

Project 5
Double Coil Bracelet
Page 27

Project 10
Bare Copper Tri-level
Bracelet
Page 32

Project 14
Tinned Copper Double-
banded Bracelet
Page 38

Project 18
Copper Coiled Bracelet
Page 44

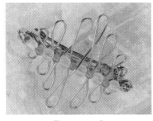

Project 19
Twisted Coil Bracelet
Page 45

Project 23
Green Cuff
Page 49

Hair Accessories and Brooches

Project 3
Beaded Blue Barrette
Page 25

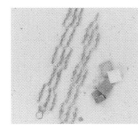

Project 16
Beaded Barrette
Page 42

Project 16
Beaded Barrette
Page 42

Project 17
Beaded Brooch
Page 43

Project 17
Beaded Brooch
Page 43

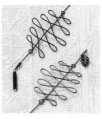

Project 26
Barrettes
Page 54

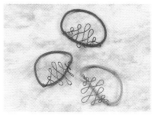

Project 29
Ponytail Holder
Page 57

Home Décor

Project 35
Easy Beaded Lampshade
Page 69

Project 36
Pillow With Wire
Charm Trim
Page 70

Project 37
Be-Dazzled Pillow
Page 71

Project 38
Tablecloth With Beaded
Fringe
Page 72

Project 39
Be-Dazzled Table Runner
Page 73

Project 40
Napkin Ring
Page 74

Project 41
Beaded Napkin Ring
Page 75

Project 42
Salt and Pepper Shakers
Page 76

Project 43
Placecard Holder
Page 77

Project 44
Wine Goblets
Page 78

Project 45
Fleur de lis Bottle
Page 79

Project 46
Flatware
Page 80

Project 47
Candleholder
Page 82

Project 48
Vase
Page 83

Project 49
Bubble Wands
Page 84

Project 50
Doggy Bone Frame
Page 86

Project 51
Ringlet Frame
Page 87

Project 52
Gift Box
Page 88

Project 53
Wired Mobile
Page 89

Paper Projects

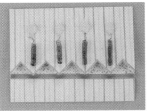

Project 54
Birthday Candles Card
Page 91

Project 55
Thanks a Whole Bunch
Card
Page 92

Project 56
Be-Dazzled Flower Card
Page 94

Project 57
Birth Announcement Card
Page 95

Project 58
Oh, Christmas Tree Card
Page 96

Project 59
Celebrate Card
Page 97

Project 60
Love Card
Page 98

Project 61
If Friends Were Flowers...
Card
Page 100

Project 62
Grape Bunch Journal
Page 101

Project 63
Sugar and Spice...
Scrapbook Page
Page 102

Project 64
Ewe Surprised Me
Scrapbook Page
Page 103

Project 65
Happy Holly Days
Scrapbook Page
Page 104

Project 66
Wedding Day Scrapbook Page
Page 105